Analyze Your Fighting

by DARIN WAUGH

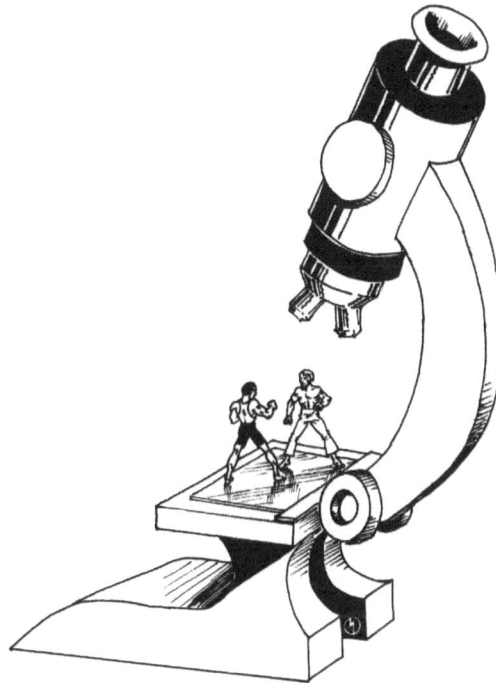

- **Analyze**
- **Strategize**
- **Execute**

Analyze Your Fighting
ISBN# 978-0-9672873-0-0

ISBN 978-0-9672873-0-0
90000

9 780967 287300

Analyze Your Fighting
by DARIN WAUGH

Table of Contents

Acknowledgments: All my past and present martial arts instructors, training partners, and students whom I've shared the "blood, sweat, and tears" of the life of a martial artist. Especially Neal Rowe (of Sacan Martial Arts pictured on the cover) who started off as my student and became my inspiration. My family who have never wavered from supporting and encouraging me. Bruce Lee, who told us it's okay to be an individual in all the traditions of martial arts and to pursue what is uniquely our own.

Preface: At some point in the early 1990's during a martial arts class being taught by Fred Karimian at The Ohio State University Do-Jung-Ishu Club, he talked about the action during an exchange of techniques between two fighters as having three stages; what happens before techniques are thrown, what happens during the exchange of techniques, and what happens after the exchange. This lecture stuck with me and eventually lead to the creation of the *Analyze Your Fighting Method (A.Y.F.M.)*. So, I'm very thankful for Fred's insight.

By looking at fighting as having three phases you're forced to be very critical about how you fight. It's this kind of "analytical thinking" that must also be used in planning your workouts.

As I collected videotaped competitions and sparring sessions, I kept more and more notes on how fighters approach fighting on a very critical level. I soon realized that I needed some practical way to organize and then interpret the information I was collecting. This lead to the creation of the analysis worksheets and then the five levels of evaluation that make up the A.Y.F.M. Now martial artists have a systematic way to understand their abilities and the complexities of fighting in a whole new way!

Kiazen Publications

Introduction

What Is The Analyze Your Fighting Method?

As a martial artist, as a fighter, how good are you, and how do you honestly answer this question in your own mind? What if someone asks you, "How good are you?" This isn't an easy question to answer. You don't want to exaggerate your skill level and sound egotistical, yet at the same time, you don't want to underestimate it either. In most cases, it's best to dodge the question all together. Undoubtedly though, the question lingers in your mind and may even dominate your training as you continue to develop more skill and confidence…and you'll keep asking yourself, "How good am I really?"

Now there is a way to know just how good you really are! By using videotaped tournament fights or sparring sessions of yourself and the ***Analyze Your Fighting Method (A.Y.F.M.),*** you can objectively determine your skill level! There is no information more valuable to you as a martial artist than knowing what skills you can use effectively or not so effectively in fighting situation!

With the A.Y.F.M. method your tournament matches and/or sparring sessions are broken down into each individual technique and movement that occurred during the fight. By doing such a comprehensive breakdown, you'll know exactly what techniques you use, how often you use them, and most importantly which ones are effective or not.

Once you have the data from your fights or sparring you can make countless comparisons between your abilities, such as how many of your techniques score as compared to how many you throw, or what percentage of your scoring techniques are punches, etc.

By analyzing your opponent you can also compare your fighting performance to your opponent's and will know exactly, in empirical terms, why you won or lost the match.

The A.Y.F.M. includes five levels of evaluation incorporating every major aspect of fighting including; identifying trends in your fighting, evaluating your attributes, analyzing the quality of your techniques, discovering your use of tactics, and assessing your mental and emotional content.

You can expect to improve your fighting from 20% - 30% after each analysis. This is based on the A.Y.F.M.'s ability to spot patterns in your fighting, which once recognized, means a quick route to improvement! The percentage of improvement is usually the result of increased efficiency in the following:

1. Number of techniques thrown.
2. The variety of techniques used.
3. More techniques scoring.
4. The quality of techniques and related attributes (speed, power, etc.).
5. The usage of tactics and strategy.
6. Improved mental focus, confidence, and decision making.

The *A.Y.F.M.* includes all the necessary instructions and worksheets to view the video and breakdown exactly what occurred during the competition or sparring match. It then teaches you how to interpret the information that you gathered from the worksheets so that you can plan effective training routines. With training that's more effective, the time it takes to increase your skill is dramatically reduced!

For example, a martial artist who moves back 75% of the time when he's attacked would do much better if he attacked more often, or learned to stand his ground and counter punch. A fighter who moves back the majority of the time is constantly on the defensive and may have problems ranging from fear, bad timing, or poor mobility. Although some people do well as "defensive" fighters, a better approach to being "defensive" is not to just wait for the attack. The "defensive" fighter should learn to move forward towards the opponent to force the opponent to attack. This keeps the opponent off-balance causing him to throw techniques when he doesn't really want to allowing the defensive fighter to use his counter skills to his advantage.

Armed with this kind of information, such as knowing that you move back 75% of the time, or that you're a defensive fighter, you and your instructor or coach can tailor your training to work on very specific aspects of your fighting ability.

To help you even more in becoming not just a good fighter but a "superior fighter," the *A.Y.F.M.* contains a chapter on planning effective workouts and another chapter on how to become a master strategist. To help you form strategies against any type of opponent, the A.Y.F.M. contains a large *Tactical Catalogue*.

After analyzing ten fights, you'll have the necessary information to determine your *Fighter's Quotient*, allowing you to compare your skill level to the *Fighters' Ability Rating Chart*. How do you rate? Are you a **Superior Fighter**?

The old saying, "knowledge is power," certainly applies to the martial arts, and the most "powerful" martial artist is the one who knows just how good he really is!

It's not so much how you play the game, it's how you analyze it, and prepare to play it again – for ultimately even if you win or lose you still have to ask why? The A.Y.F.M. is the only comprehensive program for dedicated martial artists to answer the ever-imposing questions of "how" and "why!"

If You Win or Lose You Still Have To Ask Why?

What Does An Analysis Consist Of?

The information you acquire from analyzing your fighting can radically change your approach to training! You'll have to face the truth about your fighting abilities. You don't have to rely on your own opinions or on other people's opinions as to how you perform. The analysis will clearly show the physical and mental attributes and skills that you possess and those which you're lacking in. The analysis process consists of five basic parts:

4. **VIDEOTAPING:** Have yourself videotaped during a tournament or sparring session. In order to discover the trends and patterns in your fighting, it's best to have at least three separate fights recorded. Three separate fights or sparring matches are called an **analysis block**.

2. **BREAKDOWN:** Once you have videotaped fights, use the worksheets provided in this book to "breakdown" each fight. There are three types of breakdown worksheets to log such things as technique usage, movement usage, reaction to the opponent, etc. To complete the worksheets you'll need to view each fight four different times. Each viewing of a fight is called a **pass**.

3. **DATABASE:** The *Personal Fighting Database* contains information taken from the analysis worksheets. The database is a catalog of information showing how you perform as a martial artist!

4. **EVALUATION:** Next, you'll analyze the information in the database and from other worksheets to discover the details of your fighting abilities. There are five levels of evaluation:

Level One Evaluation:	Discover and evaluate the trends in your fighting.
Level Two Evaluation:	Discover why you won or lost a particular fight.
Level Three Evaluation:	Evaluate the quality of your techniques, attributes, and tactics.
Level Four Evaluation:	Compare your fighting ability to others.
Level Five Evaluation:	Evaluate your mental control and emotional content.

5. **WORKOUT PLANNING**: The last part of the analysis process includes the planning and exaction of specific workouts and sparring sessions designed to address the weaknesses in your fighting.

The goal of doing these analyses is not just to improve your fighting, but to improve how you train. Never forget that you react in a fight the same way that you train. It's the quality of your training that determines your fighting ability! The interpretation skills that you'll develop while doing these analyses will guide you to becoming a superior fighter.

Note: *From now on throughout the rest of book the word "fight" is used to either mean a tournament fight or a sparring session.*

Impotant Analysis Terms:

Analysis Block - Is made up of either three separate sparring sessions or three tournament fights.

 Analysis Pass - A viewing of a fight on video.

Who Should Use The Analysis?

The A.Y.F.M. is not only for tournament fighters; it's just as beneficial in the martial arts school to analyze student's sparring abilities. It's applicable to any type of competition from; traditional karate tournaments, to American Boxing, to Mixed Martial Arts, to judo matches, etc.

Instructors should consider incorporating the analysis into their regular course schedule for all their students, not just those who participate in tournaments. It could even be used as part of students' rank requirements. The rate of improvement that students show is a direct result of an instructor's teaching skills and the students' level of motivation. Therefore, instructors who analyze their students will see how effective their teaching is.

Should An Instructor Charge For Doing An Analysis?

Instructors could consider charging a fee for service to do analysis and interpretation for their students. Instructors should never just look at the videotape and put together some statistics. The student must be shown how to interpret the numbers and be given detailed suggestions and guidelines on how to improve.

How Often Should An Analysis Be Done?

Analyze as often as possible. Quick improvements in skill come from knowing your weaknesses. Just being aware of a weakness in your technique is a giant step toward solving it. Most martial artists train in phases where they do a lot of sparring and then may go for a period of time when they don't spar much at all. Even the most dedicated tournament fighter has an "off season." The most beneficial time to do an analysis block (three analyses) is right before beginning a period of heavy sparring or competition to evaluate what skills need a tuned-up. Once your competition season begins the analysis should be done immediately after each tournament. This gives you the needed information to help plan your workouts as you prepare to compete again. Even if you don't compete, the analysis helps make sure that your skills are ready for sparring and self-defense.

Chapter One

Overview Of The Analyze Your Fighting Method

To establish what this system is and how it works, let's go through the process of analysis and evaluation with a brown belt karate student named James. James has been training hard and is ready to go to an open karate tournament one crisp fall Saturday morning. Along with an equipment bag full of kneepads, shin guards, and other tournament stuff, James and his instructor have brought a video camera. Someone familiar with using the video camera will carefully record each fight that James competes in. The tournament is held in a high school gymnasium, so the person doing the video recording should have no problem filming from high up in the bleachers where he/she can capture every technique.

After a long tournament day, James wins three fights and loses one, which means he placed second in his division. James and his instructor are happy with James' performance, but aren't exactly sure why James couldn't out score the last opponent to win first place. Every fight should be analyzed, but for this example, the last fight is scrutinized to discover why James lost, and to find what he needs to work on in order to become a better fighter.

After the tournament, James and his instructor prepare to analyze James' videotaped fight, by connecting the camera to the TV and with the analysis worksheets (provided at the end of the book) in hand, begin to view the fight. They will view the fight four different times (each viewing is called a "pass"). The first pass is used to document on the worksheet every technique that James threw, which arm or leg threw it (right or left), what height it was thrown at (head, body, or legs), and what happened to the technique (did it score or was it blocked, etc.). On the second pass of the video, they write down the different movements used by James during his fight, such as forward, backward, etc. During the third pass, they log how James reacted to his opponent's attacks. They view the fight a fourth time to document what technique combinations James used.

After James and his instructor finish completing the worksheets, they summarize the results. James fought a fighter two inches taller than him but only a few pounds difference in weight. They are both Shorin Ryu stylists. James threw six right leg side kicks to the midsection, none of which scored. He also threw three right leg roundhouse kicks, with one scoring. James used the following punches; nine backfists with one scoring, and four reverse punches with none scoring. He threw a total of twenty-two techniques. Two of those techniques scored giving James a scoring percentage of nine percent. James showed good bilateral use of his hand techniques by throwing an almost even amount with both his right and left arms. This is not the case with James' kicks; all of them were thrown with his right leg.

The movement breakdown revealed that James likes to move forward and to the right. James' opponent Mike threw two side kicks, four front kicks, and four roundhouse kicks. Only one front kick scored on James. His opponent also threw four backfists, four reverse punches, and two ridge hand techniques. One each of the backfist and ridgehand techniques scored, meaning James lost the fight three to two.

With the breakdown of techniques completed, James and his instructor can interpret the data they collected in many different ways. The A.Y.F.M. includes five levels of interpretation. The first level identifies the trends in James' fighting and the positive and negative effects of those trends on his performance. After completing the *Discovering Your Fighting Trends* worksheet, they found that James' side kicks aren't very effective. James doesn't use the side kick as a scoring weapon; he uses it as a way to intimidate the opponent and to keep the opponent away. He also likes to follow the side kick with a backfist, which he is able to score with. Since James is also able to score with the roundhouse kick, it would be wise if he laid off the side kick some and threw more roundhouse kicks. He may also try throwing a backfist and the side kick in combination. James threw a large number of backfists and only scored with one of them. The opponent is good at blocking backfists, but just because an opponent happens to be good at something, is never an excuse for poor performance. This is an indication of some kind of failure on James' part to overcome the opponent's strengths. James certainly is not going to have much success as a point fighter when only 10% of his backfists score. This trend needs attention! James has to learn how to score more often with his backfist.

James' instructor should examine James' backfist in more detail by looking at what occurs right before James throws the backfist, what happens during the flight of the backfist, and what happens after the technique lands or misses? Other important areas of James' techniques to analyze include; can he throw a proper technique at the proper time, can he throw the technique with strategy, is he telegraphing his techniques, etc.? The *Level Four Evaluation* addresses and evaluates these types of questions.

James' opponent, Mike, threw a slightly wider variety of techniques including front kicks and ridgehands. The ridgehand technique caught James off guard. This indicates an awareness problem that James needs to correct. Mike and James threw about the same number of techniques so one fighter really didn't dominate the other. Mike's movement pattern indicates that he likes to stand his ground and fight. James needs to recognize this type of fighter more quickly and learn to set him up. James likes to move, especially to the right when he gets in trouble. This is okay, except he needs to launch a better counter attack in these situations. You can't always run to a safe position in a fight.

Another part of the analysis (level five) that James and his instructor should take advantage of is evaluating James' thoughts, feelings, and body language as he fights. James is a nervous type of fighter. He becomes frustrated when he gets behind in points. This inhibits his ability to stay focused and to use good tactics. Using tactics and creating strategies is major part of the A.Y.F.M (chapters ten and eleven). James' main use of tactics right now is to use his side kick to set up his punches and to use his erratic movement to stay out of range. This is far from a complete "battle plan" or strategy. Learning to fight "tactically" rather than "emotionally" is the best way to become a successful fighter.

As James attends more tournaments and breaks down more fights, he'll use the *Personal Fighting Database* to log his fighting statistics. James will have a tremendous amount of information about his physical, mental, and tactical abilities. He'll use this information to design workouts that will eliminate his weaknesses while at the same time enhance his strengths.

By using the A.Y.F.M. James will have a distinct advantage over his competitors. He'll develop into a superior brown belt fighter and will undoubtedly achieve black belt sooner. At some point in the future, James can even rate his ability according to the *Fighters Ability Chart* (explained in chapter thirteen).

This overview is just a simple example of a fight analysis and what it can achieve. The rest of the book gives a detailed explanation of how to complete a fight analysis. Actually seeing a whole fight transposed into numbers gives you a whole new outlook on the martial arts. Every movement and/or technique in a fight has a history. This history contains a logical and/or emotional beginning and either a successful or an unsuccessful result. By doing the analysis you'll understand the motivation behind every technique that you use. You'll become a better thinker – and skill and knowledge are not separate entities. A skilled fighter is a knowledgeable fighter.

Outline of the Analyze Your Fighting Method (A.Y.F.M)

Step #1	View your fight(s) and complete the three technique breakdown worksheets; *Worksheets:* #1. Basic information and pre-analysis interpretation. #2. Technique usage. #3. Movement usage, Reaction to the opponent log, Combination log.

Step #2	Fill in the *Personal Fighting Database*.
Step #3	Complete the evaluation worksheets for one or more of the five levels of evaluation.
Step #4	Use the *Workout Plan* and the information you found from the evaluations to plan workouts tailored to achieving your goals.
Step #5	Use the *Strategy Worksheet* and *Tactics Catalogue* to increase your chances of winning by creating devastating strategies.

A successful analysis is not just an exercise in collecting numbers. The whole process forces you to explore what happens in a fight on many different levels. Developing the analytical ability to interpret the numbers and to see what really occurs in a fight is the ultimate goal of the A.Y.F.M. Having strong analytical skills is what separates the winners from the losers and the coach from just a martial arts instructor. All the "I'll do this" or "I'll do that" talk only strokes your ego – set your emotions aside and be objective, be real!

The following is a list of some of the analytical skills that you'll develop by doing the A.Y.F.M.:

- *Increase your understanding of the dynamics of fighting.*
- *Increase your interpretation skills.*
- *Increase your critical analysis skills.*
- *Increase your comparative analysis skills.*
- *To see usage patterns, movement patterns, reaction patterns, etc.*
- *To see your level of fighting ability, tactically, strategically, and emotionally.*

To achieve these objectives the A.Y.F.M. includes five different levels of interpretation and evaluation. In other words, each level will take you deeper into the understanding of the information that you've gathered, so that you'll no longer have to wonder, "How good am I," you'll know!

Level One Evaluation:	Discover and evaluate the trends in your fighting.
Level Two Evaluation:	Discover why you won or lost a particular fight.
Level Three Evaluation:	Evaluate the quality of your techniques, attributes, and tactics.
Level Four Evaluation:	Compare your fighting ability to others.
Level Five Evaluation:	Evaluate your mental control and emotional content.

To some people "fighting" is a primitive instinct left over from our animalistic past. Nevertheless, in the context of sports science, fighting done well is a highly involved process encompassing every possible biomechanical action and every emotion and instinct that are humanly possible. This is why there are at least five levels of evaluation when it comes to assessing the complexity of fighting.

Each level of interpretation is a fascinating exploration of fighting. You'll become a critical thinker, a scientist, and a seeker of truth – by looking at information and forming questions and opinions about how and why the information showed up. Then you'll attempt to manipulate the numbers, to define what a "better" outcome is and how to achieve it.

Using the A.Y.F.M. to become a better fighter is similar to running a corporation. The company looks at its net profit, decides it wants more profit, and then implements programs or policies to try to improve the "bottom line." After a period of time, the company will re-evaluate the results of their efforts to see if an increase in profit actually occurred. The company can also compare themselves to companies in the same industry, but ultimately success comes from constantly evaluating the company's own performance. By constantly setting goals and re-evaluating your abilities, you'll meet your potential as a fighter.

While evaluating your performance ask the appropriate questions that will lead to accomplishing your goals. For example, if your goal is to become a better kicker, than you must first define what a "better kicker" means. Does it mean that your kicks need to be faster, harder, or that you need to increase your scoring percentage with kicks, etc.? Once you've decided this, you'll determine your "base information" or where you're at now as a kicker by evaluating the information from the worksheets and database. As you continue to analyze and evaluate your kicking abilities, you'll know when you have achieved your goals.

As you work through each level of evaluation you'll develop a startling ability to not only see what you do and don't do as fighter, but will develop fantastic relational skills – the ability to see how one aspect of fighting affects all other aspects of fighting!

Suggestions For Video Taping

Unless you have recorded videotaped fights, the whole analysis process won't work. So in order to do an analysis you first must own a video camera or have access to one. The choice of a video camera is not as important as making sure every fight is recorded in its entirety and as clear as possible. The videographer needs to be familiar with the camera before he/she attempts to use it.

The best vantage point to film from is above the action, such as a balcony or the top of bleachers. Today's video cameras can usually zoom in from this distance, and deliver a nice full picture. If you're in the market for a video camera, talk to your dealer about the different types of lenses and their capabilities to zoom in and out. The best lens is one that has a 12:1 ratio. You'll also want to use a tripod. Use a tripod designed for video cameras and not for still cameras. Video tripods have a "floating head" that allows you to get a smooth panning of the action. You also want to set up so that no one can walk in front of the camera and block the action. Don't set the camera up in front of or behind the fighters – you won't get a clear shot of every technique because you'll be filming someone's back. Set up to the side of the action and keep both fighters in the picture at all times. If for some reason you can't use a tripod then try to hold the camera very still.

Once you have a good vantage point and the camera is mounted on a tripod, you're ready to film. Look through the viewfinder and place the whole fighting ring in the picture; this cuts down on the need to pan. Make sure the camera is on and recording before filming and you're on the way to using the A.Y.F.M. to become a superior fighter.

Use the list below to make sure you have all necessary equipment to videotape before you go to a tournament:

- *Pack the video camera (always guard against theft while at a tournament).*
- *Clean the lens before leaving (with lens cleaner).*
- *Charge the battery (you may consider buying an extra one).*
- *Pack the tripod.*
- *Pack a quality tape and/or memory card (bring an extra).*
- *Bring a cameraperson familiar with using the camera.*

Having yourself videotaped as you fight can be distressing, especially at tournaments. Don't feel embarrassed! You're not afraid of fighting at the tournament with hundreds of people watching, so being videotaped shouldn't be a problem. Don't let the camera being there affect your ability to fight. Be proud that you're willing to face the truth about your abilities. Improvement comes so fast by using this method that you'll soon look forward to seeing yourself on video, and whether you win or lose, you'll know you're on the path to achieving your full potential.

Analyze Your Fighting Method

Breakdown The Fight(s)

⇕

Interpret The Results

⇕

Plan Workouts Based On The Interpretations

⇕

Increase Scoring Percentages (Skill) & Winning

⇕

Re-Analyze

⇕

Superior Fighter

Your Name Here _____

Chapter Two

How To Breakdown A Fight

The ultimate goal of the A.Y.F.M. is to transform you from being a fighter who guesses and speculates about your skill, to someone who understands all the elements that make a superior fighter. The example of James and Mike is again only a simple portrayal of how much thought and interpretation can go into an analysis. This chapter will show you line by line how to complete the *Technique Breakdown* worksheets and the *Personal Fighting Database*. Remember, the analysis is not just a tool that teaches you to see what happened in a fight, it's also a device to help your interpretation skills, training evaluation, and strategy planning.

A total breakdown requires that you complete a *Pre-Analysis Worksheet* (explained later) and make four "passes" or viewings of each fight to complete the two *Technique Breakdown Worksheets*. Here's a description of what each pass involves:

Pass:	Description:
#1.	Log each technique that you threw.
#2.	Log your use of movement.
#3.	Log your reactions to the opponent's attacks.
#4.	Log your use of technique combinations.

Note: These four passes breakdown what actually occurred in the fight. To evaluate or interpret the numbers generated by the breakdown it's necessary to view the video as often as needed.

Once the breakdown worksheets are completed, than the next step in the analysis process is to start a *Personal Fighting Database*. The database stores fight statistics. It's the main interpretation tool that allows you to do the following:

- ♦ *Determine scoring percentages.*
- ♦ *Recognize technique usage patterns.*
- ♦ *Recognize effective and ineffective techniques.*
- ♦ *Recognize effective and ineffective movement patterns.*
- ♦ *Recognize effective and ineffective responses to the opponent's attacks.*
- ♦ *Recognize the use of, or lack of the use of effective fighting tactics and strategy.*

Once the weaknesses and strengths in your fighting are determined, than you'll know what training methods you should employ in order to improve your fighting. Improvements in your fighting skill are most notably reflected by the increase in your scoring percentages, or the number of techniques that score as compared to the number of techniques thrown.

Completing The Breakdown Worksheets

To perform a total fight analysis you need to complete three different types of "technique breakdown" worksheets. Each worksheet has a specific purpose and gives you a systematic approach to understanding how you fight. All the necessary worksheets are located at the back of the book (which are ready to copy). Some adaptation to the worksheets to conform to your particular style of martial art or tournament fighting may be necessary.

This chapter gives you a section by section explanation on how to complete each worksheet. The three breakdown worksheets include:

#1. Basic Information And Pre-Analysis Interpretation
#2. Technique Usage
#3. Movement, Reaction To The Opponent, Combinations

TECHNIQUE BREAKDOWN WORKSHEET #1
Basic Information & Pre-Analysis Interpretation

TECHNIQUE BREAKDOWN WORKSHEET #1
Basic Information & Pre-Analysis Interpretation

Tape #: _7_   Counter #: _454_   Analysis #: _13_

Tournament Or Sparring Session: _Central Ohio Classic_   Date: _4/7/96_

Score: Fighter #1: _3_   Fighter #2: _2_

Analysis Done By: _Mark Spencer_   Date: _4/7/96_

Fighter #1: _Mark Spencer_

School: _Hensley Karate Academy_ Style: _Shotokan_ Rank: _Brown_

Height: _5'9"_   Weight: _175_   Age: _19_

Fighter #2: _Jerry Steele_

School: _Toledo Karate Academy_ Style: _American Karate_ Rank: _Brown_

Height: _6'0"_   Weight: _177_   Age: _20_

Pre-Analysis Interpretation:

How did you feel that day before you fought? _Excited and confident!_

How did you feel about your conditioning? _Lost a week of training because of a cold._

Do you feel you were judged fairly? Why or why not? _Yes_

What is your perception of what happened? Why did you win or lose? _I lost because I couldn't beat him to the punch._

Were there noticeable differences in strength, speed, etc.? _He had very fast kicks. My punches were quicker._

What do you need to improve on? _Need to improve my ability to use counter kicks, and to be more patient. Make less mistakes!!_

What was your pre-fight strategy and did it work? _Yes it worked! I wanted to beat him to the punch and use very deceptive footwork._

Notes:
I want to workout with more fighters who have fast kicks!

Worksheet number one has two parts. The first part asks for basic information about the fight and the fighters. The second part of the worksheet is a pre-analysis interpretation. Do the pre-analysis interpretation before you view the fight(s). You do this before you begin the actual breakdown to compare what you "think" happened to what "actually" happened in the fight. You no longer want to rely on false impressions, opinions, or on exaggeration to explain how you performed.

Exaggeration can turn a nice roundhouse kick into the highest and fastest jump spinning kick ever thrown. Stay away from exaggeration. Embellishment doesn't win tournaments. Your martial arts should be rooted in truth, or what good is it? The first step in eliminating false impressions is to recognize your feelings. You want to know how you feel about your abilities – because your confidence and attitude need to keep pace with your skill development. It's not enough to know the patterns in your fighting, but you need to know the patterns in your thinking as well. Your journey to the truth in fighting begins with this first worksheet.

Completing Worksheet #1

Section #1: Organization

Tape #:   4   Counter #:   450   Analysis#:   3

This small section is important to the organization of your videotapes and the fights that are on them. Give each videotape (or whatever medium you are using) a number and clearly mark it for quick reference. Write the tournament name and date along with the index numbers on the front label of the videotape. Give each analysis a unique number. This information is important as you create analysis blocks and databases.

Section #2: Fighter Information

Tournament Or Sparring Session: *OH State Championships*   Date: *3/7/98*

Score: Fighter #1: *3*   Fighter #2: *2*

Analysis Done By: *Frank White*   Date: *3/10/98*

Fighter #1: *Tom White*

School: *Dragon's Lair*   Style: *Meibu Kai*   Rank: *Red Belt*

Height: *5'8"*   Weight: *190*   Age: *27*

Fighter #2: *Stan Caro*

School: *Kim's Karate*   Style: *Shorin Ryu*   Rank: *Brown Belt*

Height: *6'2"*   Weight: *180*   Age: *22*

This section contains general information about the tournament and the fighters who participated in the tournament – be sure to fill it out completely. You may not know all the specific information about your opponent, especially his height and weight. Go ahead and fill in the information with approximations. You may want to make a special effort to find out your competitors' names. Facing the same opponent again in the future is a real possibility. The information about your opponent's height and weight is important in determining if you're having trouble against certain body types, such as a very tall person. The analysis not only chronicles what you do as a fighter, but is a catalogue of your opponents as well.

Section #3: Pre-Analysis

Pre-Analysis Interpretation:

How did you feel that day before you fought? Fine, just normal butterflies

How did you feel about your conditioning? Good, may have over trained my legs!

Do you feel you were judged fairly? Why or why not? No, he didn't call two points!

What is your perception of what happened? Why did you win or lose? I won because my opponent

couldn't stop by kicks.

Were there noticeable differences in strength, speed, etc.? Not that I can recall without doing further analysis

What do you need to improve on? Setting up my kicks and to keep from being jammed.

What was your pre-fight strategy and did it work? I wanted to use my long reach to keep him away. I had to

Defend against his very fast backfist.

Notes:

> Analyze very carefully why opponents are able to jam my kicks so often!

Use the questions in this section to document important information that could have affected your performance. This is critical to know as you look at the breakdown numbers and begin to reflect back on your performance. For example, if you note that you were extremely nervous that day even during your fights, this would have a tremendous impact on your ability to score.

You also want to note how you felt about the judges, how an injury may have hindered you, or anything that could have had a negative impact on your performance. Keep the specifics of this kind of information in the notes section.

The pre-analysis interpretation also documents your pre-fight strategy. Great fighters know how to use strategy. Therefore, you need to be aware of how you use strategy – or even if you do! The first rule of strategy is "to know yourself" – know your own strengths and weaknesses. The whole purpose of the analysis is to "know yourself," what it is you actually do, what your habits are, and at what level you can use strategy, etc.

Once you complete the Pre-Analysis Interpretation move onto completing the technique breakdown worksheets. As you begin to evaluate your performance, refer back to the pre-analysis information for anything that may have greatly affected your performance. Do this to compare what you thought happened in the fight to what actually occurred.

> **Bring to a higher level your understanding of how you think and react during a fight.**

TECHNIQUE BREAKDOWN WORKSHEET #2
Technique Usage

Analysis #: _8_   Round(s): _1_   Fighter's Name: _CORNEAl RoWE_
Tournament Or Sparring Session: _REG. KICKBOXING CHAMPIONSHIP_   Opponent: _William WALLACE_

Breakdown Codes:

Score = S	High = (Leave Blank)	Right = R	Bad Call = BC	Jammed = JM
Penalty = P	Medium = M	Left = L	Knockout = KO	Round = \\
Warning = W	Low = X	Note = N	Terrible = T	Divides Technique = \
Counter Punch = CP	Clash = C	Faint/Fake = F	Jumping = J	Blocked = B

Punches:	Totals:	Left	Right	Right & Left	Score
1. Backfist:					
2. Reverse (Cross): L/R/RMⓈ/Rm/RⓈ/RmⓈ/R/RⓈ/R/LⓈ/R/RⓈ/		2 / 1	10 / 5	12	6 / 50%
3. Front (Jab): RⓈ/L/LⓈ/Lm/Lm/LmⓈ/L/L/L/L/L/Lm/L/L/ LF		14 / 2	1 / 1	15	3 / 20%
4. Ridge Hand:					
5. Hook L/LⓈ/L/RmⓈ		3 / 1	1 / 1	4	2 / 50%
6. Upper Cut: Rm/R/Rm/LmⓈ		1 / 1	3 / 0	4	1 / 25%
7					
8.					
Punching Totals:		20 / 5	15 / 7	35	12 / 34%

Kicks:	Totals:	Left	Right	Right & Left	Score
1. Front: Rm/Rm/Rm/Lm		1 / 0	3 / 0	4	0 / 0%
2. Side: Rm/			1 / 0	1	0 / 0%
3. Roundhouse: L/L/LF		2 / 0	0 / 0	2	0 / 0%
4. Hook: L Ⓢ /R/		1 / 1	1 / 0	2	1 / 50%
5. Crescent					
6. Spinning: Rm/			1 / 0	1	0 / 0%
7. Axe:					
8. Back Kick:					
9.					
Kicking Totals:		4 / 1	6 / 0	10	1 / 10%
GRAND TOTALS:		24 / 6	21 / 7	45	13 / 29%

Be prepared, this worksheet may send you into shock! For the first time, you'll see the reality as to what techniques you throw, how many you throw, and how often you score with them. The results of all the blood, sweat, and tears that have resulted from your martial arts training will sit before you!

This worksheet logs every kick and punch that you throw. It also tracks what happened to the technique, such as if it scored or missed, what side of the body threw it (right or left), and at what height it flew (to the head, body, or legs). After logging each technique, you'll total how many techniques you threw and then figure some statistics about your technique usage. You'll do this technique breakdown on the first viewing or "pass" of the fight.

Completing Breakdown Worksheet #2

Section #1: Codes

Breakdown Codes:

Score = S	High = (Leave Blank)	Right = R	Bad Call = BC	Jammed = JM
Penalty = P	Medium = M	Left = L	After = A	Round = \\
Warning = W	Low = X	Note = N	Terrible = T	Divides Technique = \
Counter Punch = CP	Clash = C	Faint/Fake = F	Jumping = J	Blocked = B

Use these codes on the breakdown sheet as an easy way of documenting what happened to each technique. Write the codes down on the line after the name of the technique listed under punches and kicks. Look below at the difference between a line of techniques that isn't coded and one that is:

Punches:	Tot	Left	Right	Right & Left	Score
		1	2		1
1. Backfist: Right Blocked/Right Medium/Left Scored	1	0		3	33%
		1	2		1
2. Backfist: RB\RM\L(S)	1	0		3	33%

Notice in the first example that the whole line is needed just to log three different backfists (each backfist is separated by a "\"). By using codes, as shown on the second line, more backfists fit on the line. The (S) with the circle around it means that this backfist scored. The (S) has a circle around it so that it stands out.

Section #2: Coding Techniques

The breakdown worksheet used as an explanation for this chapter has a "punches" section and a "kicks" section. For karate and kung fu styles this type of division should be adequate. For other systems of martial arts this division may not work. Feel free to either modify the worksheets contained in chapter thirteen or create your own.

The following is a detailed step by step explanation on how to use the codes to complete the worksheet.

4. Write down the names of the different punches and kicks at the beginning of the breakdown lines (unless you're using a worksheet that already lists the techniques). You can use the whole name of the technique.

2. After the technique's name, code what happened to each technique. Each technique is divided by a "\." Each technique is represented by one code or up to four codes (use the codes from the list at the top of the worksheet, or create your own set of codes). Use the following order to code the techniques.

4. The first code always identifies which arm or leg threw it – left or right.

Right = R
Left = L

b. Next, identify where the technique went.

High (no code) = To the head (leave blank)

Medium (M) = To the body
Low (L) = To the groin or legs

Note: No code is used for high, it is assumed that if "M" or "L" is not used than the technique was thrown to the head.

c. After you code for left or right and for height, than you code for what happened to the technique. Did it score? Was it blocked or jammed, etc.? There is no code for a technique that missed.

It's always assumed that the technique missed unless it's coded with an "S," in other words, a "LMS " means a left-medium technique scored, and "LMB" means a left-medium technique blocked. "LM," means a left medium technique missed.

Here is a further explanation of the codes to be sure that you understand what they represent:

B = *Blocked* – the opponent stopped the technique with his arm or leg
keeping the technique from scoring.

JM = *Jammed* – the opponent kept the technique from being completed; it was
stopped in mid-flight.

Z = *Lazy* – the technique had no real intention or energy behind it.

F = *Fake or Feeler* – a technique that is used to either test the opponent's reaction
or to set him up for an attack.

C = *Clash* – both opponents found themselves in a flurry of techniques that is
hard to decipher what happened – use this in place of breaking down each
technique that was thrown during that exchange. Use the notes section
to explain what happened.

BC = *Bad Call* – In your judgment the referee made a bad call; a technique
scored and had not been called.

\ = Divides each technique.

\\ = Divides each round.

Common Concerns That Fighters Have After Competing

1. Loss of confidence after a bad performance.
2. Believing they performed worse than they really did.
3. Believing they let their instructor, friends, or family down.
4. Not really sure what happened.
5. Overreact to something that happened.
6. Exaggerate what really happened (good or bad).

Other Coding Information To Remember

4. Whenever a technique scores put a circle around the " S " this makes it stand out more on the worksheet for easy reference.

2. There is no code for a high technique. The technique went high (to the head) if there is no "M" for medium or "L" for low used.

3. There is no code for a missed technique. It's a missed technique unless another code such as a "B" for blocked is used.

4. Make the first "pass" or viewing of the fight either in slow motion or by putting the playback device on pause after each technique. Code each technique on the appropriate line under PUNCHES or KICKS and with the appropriate codes to show what happened to the technique. Divide each technique by a "\" and each round by a "\\."

5. After reviewing and coding the whole fight, then add up the number of techniques thrown and put that number in the total column. The boxes for the left, right, and score totals have a line through them. The top half of the boxes are for the total techniques thrown, while the bottom half of the boxes are for the number of techniques that scored. Notice that there is a total for the techniques thrown with the right and left side of the body separately, and a place for the total of both right and left together. The box marked "Score" is where you write the number of times the technique scored for both right and left. The bottom of the score box is for the scoring percentage.

Kicks:	Total	Left	Right	Right & Left	Score
		3	4		2
1. Front: RMB\LM\LⓈ\RM\RP\LJ		1	1	7	29%

Here is an explanation for the codes used on the line above:

1. RMB = Right Medium Blocked
2. LM = Left Medium Missed
3. LS = Left High Score
4. RLS = Right Low Score
5. RM = Right Medium Missed
6. RP = Right Penalty
7. LJ = Left Jammed

Remember the total number of techniques goes in the top half of the box. The bottom half of the box is for writing down how many scored. There were four front kicks thrown with the right leg, and three with the left. The total of right and left equals seven, with two techniques scoring.

The bottom half of the "Score" box is for the scoring percentage, or the number of techniques thrown as compared to the number that scored. Here's an explanation of how to figure the scoring percentage:

Kicks:	Total	Left	Right	Right & Left	Score
		3	4		2
1. Front: RMB\LM\LⓈ\RM\RP\LJ		1	1	7	29%

To figure the scoring percentage for front kicks, divide the number of kicks scored into the number of kicks thrown.

Total front kicks thrown with both legs = 7
Total number of front kicks that scored = 2

Scoring percentage: $2 \div 7 = .29 \times 100 = 29\%$

This means that only 29% of this fighter's front kicks scored. Expressed as a ratio this means that about one out of every three front kicks thrown scored.

5. Repeat the first four steps for logging each technique thrown before moving onto the next worksheet.

Technique Breakdown Worksheet #3
Movement – Reaction To The Opponent – Combinations

Analysis #: _2_   Round(s): _3_   Fighter's Name: _Adam Barton_
Tournament Or Sparring Session: _Regional Kickboxing_   Opponent: _Unknown_

Movement Breakdown:

	Total			Total
Attack = //// //// //// /	16	Counter Punch (CP) = //		2
Backward (BW) = ////	4	Block Or Perry (BP) = //// /		6
Defend = //// //// /	11	Circling =		
Stoodground (SG) = ////	4	Left (L) =		
Foot Fake = /	1	Right (R) =		
Hand Fake = ///	3	Cover (CO) = /		1
Stance Switch =		Turning Away =		
Body Fake =		Spin = /		1

Reaction To The Opponent Breakdown:

Opponent: FLJ FLJ LJ LJ RMFK LJ C⑤ LRK FK FLJ RMSK
Your Reaction: CO SK⑤ BP BW BP J C⑤ SKMS FJ RC⑤

Opponent: LJ LJ⑤ LRK
Your Reaction: BW LRK

Opponent: _____
Your Reaction: _____

Notes: _____

Total Blocked: _2_   Total Avoided: _5_   Total Countered: _3_

Combination Log: RJ-/m-FK‖ RJ-LH-Rm H⑤‖ RMFK - RMSK - RC‖ RJ - RJ‖ RJ-LC
RJ-RMSK‖ RCLJ‖ RJRJ -LUC‖ RUC-LJ‖ RRK-LFK‖ RJ-LC -RH

Notes: _____

Total Hand Combinations: _7_   Total Foot Combinations: _/_   Total Hand & Foot: _3_

Technique Codes:

Back Fist = BF	Reverse Punch = RP	Cross = C	Cover = CO	Elbow = E
Jab = J	Hook = H	Upper Cut = UC	Ridge Hand = RH	Knee = K
Palm Strike = PS	Shuto = S	Forearm = FO	Shoulder = SD	Head Butt = HB
Grab = G	Roundhouse = RK	Ax Kick = AK	Back Kick = BK	Spinning Kick = Add S
Sweep = SW	Grab = G	Front Kick = FK	Side Kick = SK	Sweep = SW
Fake = F				

The third and last breakdown worksheet chronicles your use of movement, how you react to your opponent's attacks, and it also logs your technique combinations.

The second breakdown worksheet told you what techniques you threw and what happened to them. This worksheet begins to look at "how" you throw techniques by examining your movement. Techniques aren't effective without good footwork. The patterns in your techniques don't make you as vulnerable to counterattack as the patterns in your movements do!

Successful fighters are never easy targets. Therefore, the *Reaction To The Opponent* section of the worksheet logs how you responded to each one of your opponent's attacks. This allows you to discover when and how your opponents are scoring on you.

The *Combination Log* shows what techniques you use in combination. Superior fighters are capable of landing more than one technique at a time.

As you view the fight, use the pause or slow motion feature on your viewing device to log all the necessary information to complete the third worksheet.

Completing Breakdown Worksheet #3

Section #1: Movement Breakdown

After filling in the information at the top, such as the fighter's name and the analysis number, familiarize yourself with all the different movements that the worksheet tracks (see the example above). As you view the fight, mark each movement with a "1" on the appropriate line and put the total times you moved that way in the total column. For example, if you attacked ten times during the fight than the attack line would look like the example below.

Movement Breakdown:

	Total		Total
Attack = ⊬⊬⊬ ⊬⊬⊬	10	Counter Punch (CP) =	
Backward (BW) =		Block Or Parry (BP) =	
Defend =		Circling =	
Stood Ground (SG) =		Left (L) =	
Foot Fake =		Right (R) =	
Hand Fake =		Cover (CO) =	
Stance Switch =		Turning Away =	
Body Fake =		Spin =	

Most of the movement categories are easy to understand. The "stance switch" line is for those fighters who like to switch from one leg forward to the other leg forward. Use the "stood-ground" line for those times when you defend yourself without moving – you stayed in one place and blocked and/or counter attacked. Use the "cover" line when you do something such as just throwing up your arms, a leg, or an arm and a leg to defend yourself.

Section #2: Reaction To The Opponent

This breakdown takes a little more getting used to. You need to use the technique and movement codes from *Worksheet #3,* and the breakdown codes from *Worksheet #2*. Here are the steps involved in completing the *Reaction To The Opponent* portion of this worksheet.

Reaction To The Opponent Breakdown:

Opponent: _____

Your Reaction: _____

    4. View the fight and code the opponent's attacks on the opponent line.

    2. Use a down arrow (↓) to point to the "Your Reaction" line under each coded attack.

3. Code the reaction to the opponent's attack under the down arrow (↓).

Here's an example of a line not coded and one that is.

Opponent: <u>Left Medium Side Kick/ Right High Backfist/ Right Medium Roundhouse Scored</u>

Your Reaction: <u>Blocked</u>   <u>Moved Back</u>   <u>Scored</u>

Notice how the arrow from the opponent's line is pointing down to your reaction to what the opponent did. Be sure to write down when the opponent scores on you. You need to know what techniques are able to break your defense. Here's the line coded

Opponent: <u>LMSK / RBF / RMRK</u> _____

Your Reaction: <u>BP</u>   <u>BW</u>   Ⓢ _____

Section #3: Combinations

View the fight again (third pass) and study your use of combinations. Your ability to use combinations is a key ingredient to becoming a superior fighter. It's astonishing how many martial artists lack the ability to land effective combinations. The superior fighter must understand and use combinations! The use of combinations is a major key to improving your scoring percentage and chances of winning!

Combination Log: <u>BFB – JB C S // RJ – RMSK // RC – LJ // RJ – RJ – LUC LAK – RMBK // RBF</u>
<u>S</u>

<u>– MRP //</u> _____

Total Hand Combinations   __4__   Total Foot Combinations   __1__   Total Hand & Foot   __1__

To code combinations; name the techniques thrown, the height of the technique (high, medium, or low) and what happened to the technique (blocked, missed, scored, etc.). Grouped together is each technique in the combination, and each combination is divided by a "\\." Remember that, a combination is any number of techniques thrown in succession.

The first combination on the example above is BFB – JB – C S \\. This transposes into a backfist – high – blocked, jab – high – blocked, and a cross – high – scoring. If you find the codes confusing you may want to write out the whole words, such as "backfist" instead of its code BF.

Section #4: Notes

Notes: <u>I need to study how I use fakes and work on improving them!</u>_____

Use this section to document anything that happened in the fight that you may want to remember, such as how an injury occurred, or to describe how your mental attitude changed at some point in the fight. There is a "Note = N" code on *Worksheet #2.* Use "N" to refer to something that happened at a certain point in the fight that you want to describe in the notes section. For example, you may log "SKH – SKMN," which translates into, "side kick – high – side kick – medium – note." In the notes section, you might write, "I injured my ankle when I kicked the opponent's elbow and this affected my performance by keeping me from throwing anymore kicks the rest of the round."

Chapter Three

The Personal Fighting Database

Personal Fighting Database

Tournament: _X_ Sparring: _____

Analysis #	1.	2.	3.	Totals #1-3.	4.	5.	6.	Totals #4-6	Totals Blocks #1 & 2
				Block #1				Block #2	
Your Score:	3	2	3	8	2	2	3	7	15
Opponent's Score:	2	3	2	7	3	3	2	8	15
Opponent's Weight:	180	170	185		190	175	180		
Opponent's Height:	5'9"	6'2"	6'		5'9"	5'9"	6'2"		
Total Scoring Percentage Hands:	8%	11%	7%	Average 9%	0%	6%	19%	Average 12%	Average 11%
Total Scoring Percentage Kicks:	7%	0%	6%	Average 7%	12%	4%	0%	Average 5%	Average 6%
Total Punches:	12	18	15	45	8	17	16	41	86
Total Kicks:	27	30	32	89	17	24	33	74	163
Total Punches & Kicks:	37	48	47	132	25	41	49	115	247
Total Punches & Kicks Scoring Percentage:	8%	4%	6%	Average 6%	8%	5%	6%	Average 6%	Average 6%
Most Frequent Punch Name:	Back Fist	BF	BF		Reverse	BF	BF		
Most Frequent Kick Name:	Side	Side	Roundhouse		Side	Roundhouse	Front		
Movement: Attack	22	30	24	76	12	32	37	81	157
Defend	10	13	20	43	27	18	14	59	102
Fakes	7	8	12	27	4	8	12	24	51
Backwards	8	8	13	29	20	10	10	40	69
Combinations: Hand	4	3	7	14	4	5	8	17	31
Foot	3	6	6	15	4	7	6	17	32
Hand & Foot	7	9	13	29	8	12	14	34	63
Combinations Scored:	1	0	0	1	1	0	2	3	4
Reaction: Blocked	5	3	4	13	13	4	4	21	34
Avoided	1	5	11	16	10	7	4	21	37
Countered	2	2	3	7	1	4	4	9	16

*Note: Keep a separate database for tournaments and sparring.

Once you've broken down your fights by using the three breakdown worksheets, you're ready to create a database. The database keeps your information organized so that it's easy for you to study and apply to the various levels of evaluation. The *Personal Fighting Database* is the most critical part of the *Analyzing Your Fighting Method*. It's critical because, to understand how you fight you need to analyze more than one fight. The more fights that you breakdown and analyze the more accurate your interpretations become.

Since the *Personal Fighting Database* contains information about a number of fights, it makes recognizing the patterns and trends in your fighting very easy to do. This is the kind of information that's vital to planning "goal-oriented" workouts!

The database chronicles twenty-four of the most important variables in fighting as collected from the breakdown worksheets. Completing the database is a matter of using the numbers from the worksheets and putting them into the appropriate categories on the database.

After you've entered three fights, there is a space on the database for you to total all the numbers for those three fights. Analyzing and logging three fights means you've completed an "*Analysis Block.*" The next chapter explains why *Analysis Blocks* are so important and how to use them.

Completing The Personal Fighting Database

Completing the database is just a matter of finding the information from the worksheets and putting it into the proper place on the database.

TECHNIQUE BREAKDOWN WORK SHEET #1
Basic Information & Pre-Analysis Interpretation

Tape #: *14*   Counter #: *0-4028* Analysis #: *17*

Tournament Or Sparring Session: *State Championships*   Date: *12/2/97*

Score: Fighter #1: *3*   Fighter #2: *2*

Analysis Done By: *Karen Jones*   Date: *12/7/97*

Fighter #1: *Doug Salisbury*

School: *Red Dragon*   Style: *Goju-Ryu* Rank: *Brown*

Height: *5'7"*   Weight: *170*   Age: *19*

Fighter #2: *Stan Price*

School: *Smithtown Academy* Style: *Isshin-ryu* Rank: *Brown*

Height: *5'8"*   Weight: *174*   Age: *21*

The information for the first four columns of the database will come from the portion of *Worksheet #1* shown above. Here's how the information will look in the database.

Personal Fighting Database

Tournament: __X__   Sparring: _____

Analysis #	1.	2.	3.	Block #1 Totals #1-3.	4.	5.	6.	Block #2 Totals #4-6	Totals Blocks #1 & 2
Your Score:	3								
Opponent's Score:	2								
Opponent's Weight:	174								
Opponent's Height:	5'8"								

The information for the next eight columns of the database will come from *Worksheet #2* (Technique Usage) as shown below. *Note: See the sample of Worksheet #2 on page thirteen.*

				Average				Average	Average
Total Scoring Percentage Hands:	34%								
Total Scoring Percentage Kicks:	10%			Average				Average	Average
Total Punches:	35								
Total Kicks:	10								
Total Punches & Kicks:	45								
Total Punches & Kicks Scoring Percentage:	29%			Average				Average	Average
Most Frequent Punch Name:	Jab								
Most Frequent Kick Name:	Front								

Be sure to put the right numbers in the correct place. The *Technique Breakdown Worksheet* contains the totals for punches, kicks, and punches and kicks combined, as well as scoring percentages. Remember, the scoring percentages are very important because these are the numbers that you want to improve. A superior fighter has a very high scoring ratio, meaning that almost every technique he throws scores!

The information for the remaining twelve blocks of the database comes from *Worksheet #3* (movement, reactions, and combinations) as shown below:

Movement Breakdown:

	Total		Total
Attack = ⅌⅀ ///	8	Counter Punch (CP) = ⅌⅀	5
Backward (BW) = ⅌⅀ /	6	Block Or Parry (BP) = ⅌⅀ ///	8
Defend = ⅌⅀ ⅌⅀ ⅌⅀ /	16	Circling = //	2
Stood Ground (SG) = ///	3	Left (L) = ⅌⅀	5
Foot Fake = ⅌⅀ ////	9	Right (R) = ///	3
Hand Fake = //	2	Cover (CO) = //	2
Stance Switch = /	1	Turning Away =	
Body Fake =		Spin =	

Combination Log: RJ – LM – FK // RJ – LH – RM H(S) // RMFK – RC // RJ – RJ //

RJ – LC – RJ – RMSK // RCLJ // RJ – RJ – LUC // RUC – LJ //

RRR – LFK // RJ – LC – RH

Total Hand Combinations = 6   Total Foot Combinations = 1   Total Hand & Foot = 3

Movement: Attack	8									
Defend	16									
Fakes	11									
Backwards	6									
Combinations: Hand	7									
Foot	1									
Hand & Foot	3									
Combinations Scored:	1									
Reaction: Blocked	8									
Avoided	8									
Countered	5									

Complete the movement portion of the database by using the information from the movement section of *Worksheet #3*. Notice that only some of the information from the movement section becomes part of the database. The database tracks the most important movements, such as how often you attack as compared to defending yourself. Other movement information that is not a part of the database is still important. Use that information to make specific evaluations of your movement skills. For example, you may find that you have a tendency to move to the right most of the time as you fight. You'll want to discover why you move to the right and if your opponents can take advantage of it, etc.

Use the combination portion of the worksheet to complete the remaining blocks of the database. Remember, the superior fighter understands how important it is to have the ability to score with combinations.

Database Analysis Blocks

An "analysis block" is the total numbers from three fights or three sparring sessions. The column marked *Block #1* contains the numbers for the first analysis block. Notice after the first six fights there are two blocks, one for the totals from fights four through six, and the next for totaling the numbers from analysis blocks one and two. This is the total for your first six fights.

Analyzing one fight gives you information about that fight. Analyzing a "block of fights" is what gives you information about trends and patterns in your fighting. Always strive to videotape in "analysis blocks" (three separate fighting sequences) whenever possible. You can use three rounds of two minutes to equal one sparring match. This means you would do three sparring matches of three two-minute rounds to make one *Analysis Block*. You can do this in any combination of ways, but make sure there are breaks and a rest period in-between each sequence, and either use three different opponents or keep the same one for the whole block of fights. Using the same fighter twice and a different fighter for the third sparring match will create inconsistency in your numbers. Tournament fights already have time limits built into them, so there's no problem analyzing each fight. You may want to use the same timed rounds and time between rounds in your sparring that are used in the competition that you're training for.

Don't be afraid to be creative with your analyses and your databases. You may want to log each fight in rounds on the database instead of each fight individually. You may decide to create analysis blocks with four or five fights. Just remember to keep separate databases for your sparring and your competition.

Analysis blocks not only summarize your fighting, but also allow you the opportunity to compare "blocks of fights." The more fights you analyze the more accurate the interpretation of your skills become.

Use the information from the breakdown worksheets
and/or Personal Fighting Database
to create graphs and charts!

Creating Graphs & Charts

You can use charts and graphs as another way to illustrate your performance statistics. The statistics that you use can come from any of the breakdown worksheets and *Personal Fighting Database*.

There are many types of graphs and charts, the following examples are some of the most common.

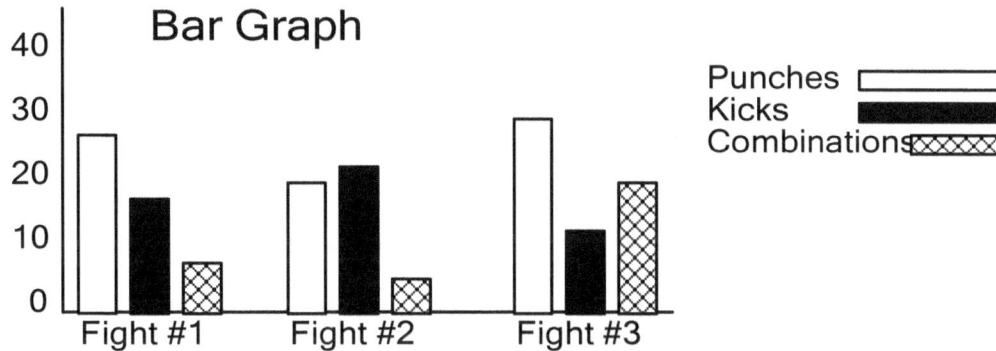

Bar Graph

This bar graph shows how many punches, kicks, and combinations that this fighter used over three fights. This fighter is interested in figuring out why he has such inconsistency in his technique usage. It could be that he is successfully adapting to different opponents or perhaps he's fighting according to how he feels that day, etc.

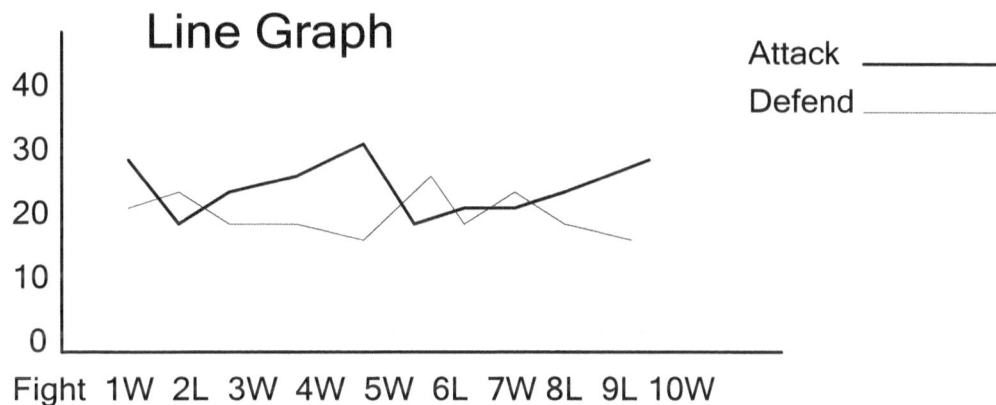

Line Graph

This line graph clearly shows that this fighter is more likely to win when he attacks more than he defends. Why is this true? Perhaps, when he's attacking he's controlling the pace of the fight and is more aggressive than his opponent. Or maybe, he's losing against fighters that are more aggressive than he is?

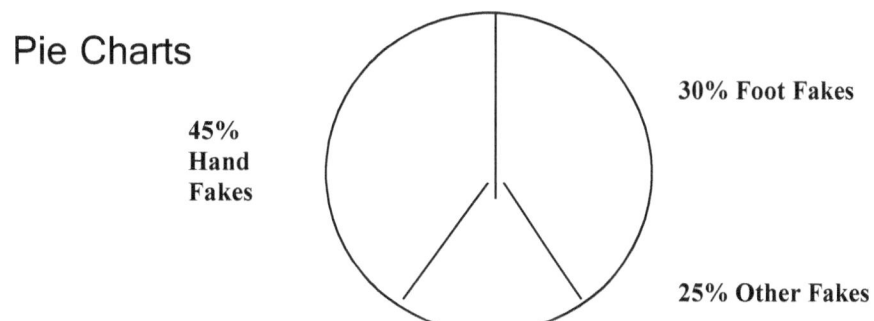

Pie Charts

45% Hand Fakes

30% Foot Fakes

25% Other Fakes

This pie chart shows that this fighter makes good use of many different types of fakes. He should keep it up!

28

Chapter Four

Level One Evaluation

"To win against one opponent is the same thing as winning against thousands or tens of thousands of opponents."

Miyamoto Musashi

Discovering Trends In Your Fighting

Now that you know how to complete the breakdown worksheets and the *Personal Fighting Database;* throw out any speculation about how you really fight as if it's old sparring equipment! You're ready to interpret the information you collected from the breakdown worksheets so that you can design specific workouts and training routines that will procure your status as a superior tactician, strategist, and fighter!

Every example given in this book has come from real numbers gathered from point karate tournaments or from real dojo sparring sessions. Since they are actual numbers, you should already be wondering about such things as your own technique frequency (how many techniques you throw) and technique variety (how many different techniques you use). You should also be very surprised to find that the majority of techniques thrown never hit the opponent and that most fighters only use four or five different techniques on a regular basis. Consider all the training that fighters do just to develop the ability to really land (or score with) four or five different techniques! Why is this true, and what should fighters do in order to change this? You're going to conquer these questions and many more like them as you learn to interpret the results of your analyses.

Level I Evaluation: Recognizing Trends

Use the *Personal Fighting Database* to complete the level one evaluation. The database logs the most obvious aspects of your performance and clearly shows the trends in your fighting.

Discovering Your Fighting Trends
Level One Evaluation

Trend Evaluation:

(Behavior) and/or comparison: _Scoring percentage of kicks._

Time period or number of fights: _6 Fights_

Frequency: _Kicks were 11% of the total techniques that scored._

Positive or negative affects of this trend on performance: _limited scoring ability with kicks. Opponent's will know I'm not an effective scorer with kicks_

Goal(s) for improving or changing this trend:
1. _Improve scoring percentage with kicks from 11% to 28%_
2. _Accomplish the above in three months_
3.
4.

Training ideas & notes:
Study videotapes of fighters who are effective kickers.
Have my instructor design kicking drills for me.
Workout with Mike, he's a great kicker!

Trend Evaluation:

Behavior and/or comparison: *Compare how movement affects defense*

Time period or number of fights: *3 Fights*

Frequency: *Stood ground 69% / Counter punch 20% / Other movement 11%*

Positive or negative affects of this trend on performance: *Not making good use of movement while defending. Standing still and trying to block or counter punch too often. Need to be more of a moving target. Need to learn to counter punch while moving.*

Goal(s) for improving or changing this trend: *Achieve the following in six months*

1. *Learn to move and counter punch.*
2. *Learn how to cause the opponent to miss with movement*
3. *Reduce standing around from 64% of the time to below 40%*
4. *Increase all other movement from 11% to above 30%*

Training ideas & notes:

Research how other fighters and styles use footwork. Study boxing footwork and footwork drills.

First, you must understand what a trend is so that you can spot them on the database. A trend is made up of three factors; the behavior you're observing (such as a front kick), the frequency of the front kick (how many you threw), and a given time period in which front kicks occurred (such as an analysis block which is three fights).

Trends are also associated with desirable and undesirable results. A desirable or "good" trend is the tendency for a technique, tactic, or strategy to score on an opponent. An undesirable trend is the lack of ability to respond to the opponent's technique, tactic, or strategy. In other words, anything that allows opponents to score on you. Therefore, it's of paramount importance that you know all your "trends" both good and bad. You want to know your good trends, or the things that you do well, so that you can make them stronger and more consistent. You want to know your negative trends, those things that cause you to be beaten, so you can eliminate them.

It's also important to recognize the skills and techniques that you "don't do" or hardly ever use. Be sure that adding new skills is a constant part of your training.

Trends occur for many reasons, the most influential is what "style" or system of martial arts you study and how you train. Certain styles have a tendency to use certain techniques and to employ certain tactics. The other obvious reasons for why trends occur are due to personal likes and dislikes.

As you go through the process of analyzing for trends, think of yourself as a behavioral scientist –and you're the subject of study. Ask yourself these two basic questions, "How come I do that?" and "How come I don't do that?" Keep analyzing your data and reviewing your fights until you come up with satisfactory answers.

How To Analyze For Trends

In analyzing for trends, you're primarily studying what it is that you do and don't do consistently over a number of fights. This is different from discovering why you won or lost a particular fight. To answer that question, you'll analyze that particular fight and do a complete breakdown for both you and your opponent. Chapter six explains how to analyze why you won or lost a particular fight. For now, it's important to know how you perform over a number of fights, not just one fight, in order to adjust your training so that you can become a more successful fighter.

There comes a point in your career as a fighter where examining individual fights is more beneficial to you. This comes after you've competed for several years and have a clear knowledge of how you fight and what type of fighter you are. When you first begin to analyze how you fight, it's the "obvious" adjustments that will make huge differences. These "obvious" negative factors show up as trends!

As explained earlier, a trend has three basic elements; a behavior that is being observed or recorded, the frequency of the behavior, and a time period in which the behavior occurs. Therefore, a trend (or behavior) is easy to recognize just by looking at the results of several fights on the database. This is why the database contains "analysis blocks," you can't accurately identify a trend from only one fight.

The following lists the most common types of positive and negative trends:

Positive Trends: **Negative Trends:**

Positive Trends	Negative Trends
Increase in winning.	Lose more than you win.
Increase in scoring percentage.	Poor mobility
Increase in variety of techniques used.	Ineffective use of combinations.
Increase in use of technique combinations.	Poor mental focus.
Consistent positive and focused attitude.	Ineffective use of tactics and strategy.
Increase in the use of tactics and strategy.	Poor technique quality (telegraphing, etc.)
Etc.	Low scoring percentages.
	Etc.

Completing The Trend Analysis Worksheet

The *Level I Evaluation For Trends* is not difficult to perform. The scope of it can be somewhat overwhelming once you begin to compare how one trend in one area of fighting such as kicking, affects the trends in another area, such as how you move.

The following examples show how you can easily understand the trends in your fighting. The first example illustrates only one aspect of fighting, while the second compares two different aspects of fighting.

Level One Fighting Trends: *Example One*

Trend Evaluation:

Behavior and/or comparison: _Scoring percentage with kicks_

Time period or number of fights: _6_

Frequency: _Average of 13% scoring percentage with kicks_

Positive or negative affects of this trend on performance: _I have limited scoring ability with my kicks. Opponents will know I don't score well with kicks. I don't want to be a fighter who has limited kicking abilities!_

Goal(s) for improving or changing this trend:
1. _To double my scoring percentage with kicks from 13% to 26%._
2. _Achieve the above in 9 months._
3.
4.

The first example focuses on this fighter's scoring percentage with kicks. Over the course of six fights, he achieved a thirteen-percent scoring percentage with kicks. That means that eighty seven percent of his scoring techniques were punches. This fighter clearly prefers to score with punches rather than kicks.

By doing this analysis for trends, this fighter recognizes that he has limited scoring ability with kicks, and his opponents are taking advantage of it. Therefore, he sets as his goal to double the scoring efficiency of his kicks from thirteen percent to twenty-six percent. Notice that he also includes a time limit to achieve his new goal.

Use the notes section to document any thoughts, questions, training ideas, etc., that you have as you complete the evaluation. Don't be afraid to keep extensive notes and to refer to these notes while planning your workouts.

Ask yourself these questions as you think about the trends you're evaluating:

1. Do you use it and how often?
2. Does it score or not and how often?
3. Do you use it in combination with other things and how often?
4. How does it contribute to you losing?
5. What effect does it have on your ability to win?
6. Etc.

Level One Fighting Trends: *Example Two*

Trend Evaluation:

Behavior and/or comparison: *How my movement patterns affect my defense.*

Time period or number of fights: *9*

Frequency: *Defended 156 times; moved back (97); moved rt (10) moved left (4) Stood ground (45)*

Positive or negative affects of this trend on performance: *Moved back 62% of the time. This means I'm running from the opponent alot. I only move right or left 9% of the time. Opponent's will know I don't use lateral movement.*

Goal(s) for improving or changing this trend:

1. *Change my movement patterns while defending to the following*
2. *Move back under 50% of the time*
3. *Move right a left 20% of the time*
4. *Achieve the above in 6 months*

This trend evaluation shows how you can compare two different parts of the database to see how one area of fighting affects another. In the above example, this fighter examined how his movement patterns affects his defense.

Compare as many different elements as you want by simply picking two different categories from the personal fighting database. Be specific in your notes on how you feel about the comparisons. Remember, the next step is to find ways to improve what you find wrong with your abilities.

There are some circumstances where you'll want to refer back to the technique breakdown worksheets – when the database doesn't have the information you want. Such a circumstance could occur when you want to look at what specific techniques you're throwing as compared to which ones you're not throwing. For example, you may want to look at how many front kicks you're using as compared to side kicks. Study the following list for more comparison ideas:

1. Tendency to use which hand and foot combinations with fakes?
2. Tendency to use which punches and kicks in reaction to the opponent's attack?
3. Tendency to use which blocks or parries against attacks?
4. Tendency to use foot combinations as compared to hand combinations?
5. Tendency to use what type of techniques to score against tall opponents?
6. Tendency to use what type of movement to set up attacks?
7. Tendency to be mentally confident until what occurs?
8. Tendency to have difficulty scoring against what type of fighter?
9. Tendency to not be able to adjust to what kind of defense by the opponent?
10. Tendency for what techniques to score on you?
11. Etc.

Trends ultimately tell what you know how to do and don't know how to do in a fighting situation – they are what determine your skill level!

Trends In Scoring

The whole purpose of tournament competition is to win by outscoring your opponent (or in some cases to knock him out). Scoring on an opponent, however defined by the tournament rules such as light contact, full contact, or mixed martial arts is the accumulation of all the variables in fighting. Scoring is a test of volition – the culmination of training and response! **Scoring on the opponent is the highest order of action!** All the other variables in combat such as speed, timing, technique selection, etc. affect your ability to score. It stands to reason then, that any act of training, or desire to be a good puncher or to be faster, etc., is for the goal of being more effective at scoring. In other words, it's never enough to want to be a "good puncher" the punches have to land on a moving opponent. You should judge something "good" or "effective" as being directly related to how often you can score with it! This is what the A.Y.F.M. is designed to do – not to tell you what is "good," but to help you discover what "good" is in terms of your own martial arts experience.

The scoring percentage defines your ability to score. It's a different level of thinking to say to yourself, "I score with 60% of my punches," rather than saying, "I'm a good puncher." Until there are true scientific studies done on what effectiveness means in the martial arts, you'll need to judge what effectiveness means to you. Base effectiveness on your true ability to score – look at what techniques you score with and how often you score with them.

There are four different ways in which the *Personal Fighting Database* logs information about scoring;

1. Score – how many points you scored.
2. Total scoring percentage of punching techniques.
3. Total scoring percentage of kicking techniques.
4. Total scoring percentage of punching and kicking techniques together.

The score itself is a record of your success. Its primary use is in keeping track of your win/loss record at tournaments. Out scoring your opponents in sparring sessions isn't as important as using your time sparring to increase your ability to score (which will increase your scoring percentages in competition). Knowing as much as possible about how you score, what you score with, and what keeps you from scoring should be your number one goal as a competitive fighter!

Limits On Scoring

Unless you're fighting in a situation where there are no rules, there are limits on your opportunity to score in competition, or you'll face disqualification. Sometimes you're limited to a set score, such as in a point karate tournament, in which the first person to score three points wins. Other types of tournaments have timed rounds with scoring limited to the amount of time in each round (such as kick-boxing). Body targets are limited in tournaments for safety reasons, as well. Even the degree of contact allowed and safety equipment used, are going to affect your opportunity to score. Sparring with your fellow students in your dojo (school) is done with some kind of limits on what you can do, also.

If your martial arts style emphasizes one aspect of fighting over another, than your numbers on the *Personal Fighting Database* will reflect the style's preferences. For example, if your style emphasizes punches over kicks, the database will show a higher usage percentage and scoring percentage with punches as compared to kicks. If your style doesn't place an emphasis on one aspect of fighting over another, then the differences in these numbers will reflect your natural personal preferences.

Try to avoid having a technique preference that is out of balance. Throwing three times more hand techniques than foot techniques is a trend that some opponents can easily exploit. Ideally, you don't want your opponent to be sure whether or not you're going to throw a kick or a punch. You want them to feel threatened by as many weapons as possible.

Use the notes section to explain why your use of hand techniques and foot techniques are the way they are, and what you might do to correct any imbalance between them. Keep this in mind as you go onto the next level of evaluation.

Your ability to score is also dependent upon the skill level of your opponents or sparring partners. It's more difficult to score against someone who is at a higher skill level. Sparring against those who are better than you is a necessary part of training. It's the more skilled martial artists who will pull you up to higher levels (provided your training and sparring sessions are geared towards learning). Even when sparring someone of a higher level try very hard to maintain your scoring percentage. You'll be out scored, but remember, that scoring percentage depends on how many techniques you throw and can score with. Be aggressive and confident; find a way to score. Keep your scoring percentage consistent or constantly improving no matter who you're sparring.

Keep the same intensity to score in sparring as you do in competition. Don't use the same sparring partners all the time. Spare with practitioners from as many different martial arts styles as you can. The scoring percentage that you achieve while sparring against those of your same rank is your true gauge of success.

Despite the restrictions on your opportunity to score, such as rules and the skill level of your opponent, most limits on scoring are self-inflicted – dependent on the mental and physical limitations that you haven't yet overcome. There's a distinct difference between training to learn a skill and training to score.

Examples Of Scoring & Win/Loss Records

Here are two different sets of scoring results taken from a *Personal Fighting Database*. The first example is from a series of sparring sessions, and the second is from a series of point karate tournaments.

Trends In Sparring Scores:

Trend Evaluation:

(Behavior) and/or comparison: *Scoring percentage during sparring*

Time period or number of fights: *3*

Frequency: *Scoring percentages for first three fights; 11%, 39%, 18%*

Positive or negative affects of this trend on performance: *Scoring percentage jumps around — not consistent. Average scoring percentage is around 30% this isn't very high. A low scoring percentage means most of my techniques aren't scoring*

Goal(s) for improving or changing this trend:

1. *Increase my scoring percentage to 50%*
2. *Keep my scoring percentage consistent*
3. *Discover why I'm having so much trouble scoring*
4. *Create training routines that will increase my scoring %*

Training ideas & notes:

This first trend evaluation shows that there is a clear inconsistency in scoring percentage. The highest percentage of 39% shows that this fighter has the potential to reach a high percentage, but why the low percentages such as 11% or 18%? Expressed as a ratio that means that only one or two techniques out of ten score. This person could not be a successful tournament fighter with such a low scoring percentage unless he has a terrific defense.

Trends In Tournament Scores:

Trend Evaluation:

(Behavior) and/or comparison: *Scoring % during tournaments*

Time period or number of fights: *3*

Frequency: *Scoring percentage average = 27%*

Positive or negative affects of this trend on performance: *A low scoring percentage translates into a low winning record. I'm not an effective scorer. A low scoring will mean I can't achieve my goals*

Goal(s) for improving or changing this trend:

1. *To maintain a scoring percentage of 30-40%*
2.
3.
4.

Training ideas & notes:

Further investigate why I have such a low scoring percentage. Do a level three evaluation.

The fighter's goal in this example is to win 75% of his tournament fights. His current average scoring percentage is 27%. To meet his goal, he realizes that he needs to maintain an average scoring percentage of 30% - 40%. He understands the need to increase his scoring percentage in order to win more fights. He also reminds himself in the notes section to further his investigation into why he has such a low scoring percentage. With further investigation he may find that he's too much of a defensive fighter, or that his techniques are not well timed, etc.

Conclusion

By studying the trends in your fighting, you're examining how what you do or don't do affects your ability to score. Ideally, you want to show a steady increase in your scoring percentage. That is, it doesn't matter if as a result of your training you throw more techniques in a fight, or you become a more conservative fighter and use fewer techniques (but pick them more carefully), you still want to increase your scoring percentage. A high scoring percentage means that with each technique you throw it's more likely to score. This is the "impact" of a great fighter!

Chapter Five

Level Two Evaluation

"A fighter must not only know when to hit, but when not to hit – fighting involves many things."

Fred Karimian

Winning Or Losing A Particular Fight

The *Level II Evaluation* is a way for you to discover why you won or lost a particular fight. Instead of looking at a series of fights (such as an analysis block) like you would in discovering trends in your fighting, now you'll examine one particular fight. Perhaps, you did your best in a fight for first place but still lost and want to know the reasons why. Maybe you won a very challenging match against a well-known opponent and you want to find out specifically why you won. Completing a *Level II Evaluation* helps you find the reasons why you won or lost. As with any conclusions made from any level of evaluation it's your goal to incorporate the information from the *Level II Worksheet* into planning your training sessions.

There are two different methods to doing a *Level II Evaluation*. The first method is not as detailed as the second. The first method requires that you only view the videotaped fight and complete the *Level II Worksheet*. The second method is a more involved evaluation because you also incorporate information from any or all of the levels of evaluations or worksheets offered in this book.

Your key to success in doing this level of evaluation is to keep your thoughts organized, and to use good observational skills that will lead to an increased understanding of your abilities and the dynamics of fighting in general.

Before going on to complete the *Level II Worksheet,* you should understand the importance of viewing the fight to discover the following: (1) who controlled the pace of the fight, (2) who controlled the distance, and (3) who showed a dominant strategy.

Controlling The Pace

Each fight has a unique rhythm. This rhythm is the timing of the exchange of techniques between the combatants and the time between exchanges (when the fighters are stalking each other looking for the right moment to attack). Usually, the rhythm or timing of the fight is controlled by the more aggressive fighter (the fighter who attacks more often than he defends). He takes the initiative. He forces the opponent to react to him. He wants control. Other fighters are more comfortable with waiting for the opponent's attack. Two aggressive fighters competing against each other will usually produce a very fast paced fight with lots of action. Two defensive or counter types of fighters competing together will produce a much slower fight as each fighter waits for the other to attack.

Usually, the fighter who controls the pace of the fight, is the fighter who wins. If you control the pace of the action than you're also controlling when you score. You may try slowing down the aggressive fighter by beating him to the punch or by using elusive footwork while maintaining your ability to fire a scoring technique. Or, you may force a cautious fighter to feel uncomfortable by using lots of exaggerated movement and hitting from strange angles. No matter what you do, you won't dominate your opponents until you control the pace of the fight. **By controlling the pace, you force the opponent to fight your fight, according to your tactics.** You transform the fight from just being a bunch of random acts into a pattern where you're continually setting your opponents up to be scored on.

Controlling The Distance

Along with controlling the pace of a fight, it's also important to control the distance between you and your opponent. You want to be where you can score according to your attributes and tactical choices. You want to keep the opponent at the optimal distance and set him up for your attack. Use a distance that is comfortable to you but uncomfortable to the opponent.

To control the distance you must have exceptional footwork. You should never be moving around just for the sake of moving (some fighters just bounce around for no apparent reason), every movement should have a reason.

Dominant Strategy

Tactics and strategies are explained in greater detail in chapters seven and eleven, but it's important in the level two evaluation to recognize when someone is using a "dominant-strategy." A dominant-strategy is a very obvious plan for winning a fight. For example, if someone is a very powerful puncher and he's trying to take his opponent's head off during the whole fight, then he's using a dominant strategy. He's using his strength to his advantage. Another fighter may have a very fast and powerful left leg, his dominant strategy is to do everything he can think of to set his opponents up for left leg kicks.

As you do this level of evaluation, pay attention to how "dominant strategies" contributed to you winning or losing the fight.

How To Complete A Level Two Evaluation: Method I

The first method for determining why you won or lost a particular fight relies mostly on observation. That is, you simply view the fight and answer the questions on the worksheet. You'll list the positive and negative aspects of your performance in five different areas of fighting including; body type, attributes, technique usage, mental skills, and tactical knowledge. These five basic areas of fighting form the foundation for the whole A.Y.F.M., and are examined in detail throughout the book. Here's a simple definition of each one of these areas:

Body Type - the physical description of a fighter, whether he is tall, short, heavy, etc.

Attributes - a fighter's talent or lack of talent in such areas of fighting as; speed, power, timing, mobility, precision, endurance, focus, recovery, etc.

Technique Usage - what techniques a fighter uses and those which he doesn't use and how well he uses them.

Mental Skills - how well a fighter; controls his emotions, can stay focused on winning, controls his fears, handles stress, etc.

Tactical Knowledge - how well a fighter can use techniques and tactics in order to set up his opponents; and how well he chooses certain techniques and tactics to adapt to the constantly changing aspects of the fight, etc.

Completing The Level Two Worksheet: Method I

The worksheet contains eight questions. Your main objective is to conclude why you won or lost a fight by listing and comparing the positive and negative aspects of your performance. Study the example below to see the correct way to complete the worksheet. Pay particular attention to how the conclusion is a literal summary of the observations made about the fight. The conclusion also helps create training ideas. Also, notice the suggestions for further analysis in the notes section.

Winning Or Losing A Particular Fight
Level Two Evaluation

Tape #: _3_   Counter #: _459_   Analysis #: _17_

Fighter #1: _Don Scott_   Score: _1_
Fighter #2: _Ron Bueller_   Score: _3_

1. This evaluation is being done to discover why you: A.) Won ____ B.) Lost _X_ C.) Other ____

_____

2. List the positive and negative aspects of your performance in each of the categories below:
(Use another worksheet if you wish to list these aspects of your opponent's performance.)

Body Type: Positive
1. I'm 3" taller than Ron
2.
3.

Body Type: Negative
1. Ron out weighes me by 10 lbs.
2. He has very strong legs
3.

Attributes: Positive
1. Good hand speed
2. Didn't become tired
3. Longer reach
4. Had good footwork
5.

Attributes: Negative
1. Not as physically strong
2.
3.
4.
5.

Technique & Tactic Usage: Positive
1. Beat him to the punch
2. Good defense against his hands
3. Scored with one reverse punch
4. I controlled the distance
5.

Technique & Tactic Usage: Negative
1. Couldn't stop his kicks
2. He controlled the pace
3. He constantly tried to come in on me.
4. I didn't throw any combinations
5. He kept me off balance w/ his kicks

Mental Skills: Positive
1. Never gave up
2. Had good focus
3.
4.
5.

Mental Skills: Negative
1. Became apprehensive against his kicks
2. Wasn't aggressive enough
3.
4.
5.

3. Did your fight strategy work? Why or why not?
I wanted to use my greater reach and hand speed to land punches but he worked cover up and use his strong kicks.

4. Who controlled the pace and why?
He did because he kept coming at me

5. Who controlled the distance and why?
I controlled the distance with my quicker footwork but failed to really take advantage of it.

6. Conclusion as to why you won, lost, or other?
His kicks were too strong for my defense. He scored all three of his points with kicks. I had no effective strategy against his kicks.

7. Training ideas and/or notes:
Need to research and practice tactics against strong kicks. Use the Analyze Your Fighting Tactics Catalogue.

In the preceding example, Don wants to discover why he lost to Ron in a karate point tournament. You can see that Don lost the fight by two points. As you look over the answers written in each category under question two, it becomes very apparent that Don found his opponent's kicks to be very overwhelming. He failed to adapt to Ron's aggressive kicking tactics. Although Ron had faster hands than Don, Don kept Ron off balance by bombarding him with hard kicks. Don did score with one reverse punch, but couldn't put together any kind of combinations or effective counters to Don's kicks.

Don's fight strategy (question three) of trying to use his greater hand speed failed because Ron would cover up and keep blasting kicks. Ron controlled the pace of the fight because he kept coming at Don (question four) even though Don controlled the distance with his quick footwork. Controlling the distance didn't help Don since he couldn't really set Ron up for anything, and Don found himself continually blocking kicks.

Don came to the logical conclusion that he failed to adapt to his opponent's strong kicks and that's why he lost the fight. In the training and notes section of the worksheet, Don says that he needs to research and practice tactics against strong aggressive kickers.

Completing The Level Two Worksheet: Method II

The worksheet used in *Method II* is exactly the same one as in *Method I*. The only difference between the two methods is that *Method I* is done by observing the fight and completing the worksheet, while *Method II* incorporates information from other evaluation worksheets and the *Personal Fighting Database*.

You'll choose how in-depth you want to study your performance and the performance of your opponent. For example, you may decide to do a complete technique breakdown of you and your opponent to see exactly what both of you scored with. Or perhaps, you want to study the "quality" of the techniques used by you and your opponent. There are countless ways to add detailed information to the worksheet to make a more complete and accurate evaluation.

Notice how the detail in the example below is more explicit than in the first example. Pay attention to the empirical data. Also, notice that the notes section lists the worksheets used to help complete the evaluation.

Winning Or Losing A Particular Fight
Level Two Evaluation

Tape #: _3_   Counter #: _459_   Analysis #: _17_

Fighter #1: _Don Scott_   Score: _1_
Fighter #2: _Ron Bueller_   Score: _3_

1. This evaluation is being done to discover why you: A.) Won ____ B.) Lost _X_ C.) Other ____

2. List the positive and negative aspects of your performance in each of the categories below:
(Use another worksheet if you wish to list these aspects of your opponent's performance.)

Body Type: *Positive*
1. I'm 3" Taller than Ron
2.
3.

Body Type: *Negative*
1. Ron out weighs me by 10 lbs.
2. He has very strong legs
3.

Attributes: *Positive*
1. Good hand speed
2. Didn't become tired
3. Longer reach
4. Had good footwork
5.

Attributes: *Negative*
1. Not as physically strong
2.
3.
4.
5.

Technique & Tactic Usage: *Positive*
1. Beat him to the punch but only
2. Scored once (reverse punch)
3. I controlled the distance
4.
5.

Technique & Tactic Usage: *Negative*
1. Opponent attacked 20 times I attacked only 7
2. Opponent threw 9 combinations I scored
3. I only used 3 combinations all hands
4. My scoring % = 20% Opponent's scoring % = 45%
5. I had no defense against his kicks

Mental Skills: *Positive*
1.
2.
3.
4.
5.

Mental Skills: *Negative*
1.
2.
3.
4.
5.

3. Did your fight strategy work? Why or why not?
No. I wanted to use my greater reach to use interception techniques to score on him. Of the opponent's 20 attacks I attempted 8 interceptions only scoring with one. I had no defense against his kicks.

4. Who controlled the pace and why?
He did because he kept coming at me. He attacked almost three times more than I did.

5. Who controlled the distance and why?
I did because of my quicker footwork but couldn't take advantage of it because of his strong kicks.

6. Conclusion as to why you won, lost, or other?
I had no effective strategy against his strong kicks. His scoring percentage was two times higher than mine.

7. Training ideas and/or notes:
Technique breakdown worksheet
Level three evaluation

This example includes more statistics about the fight between Don and Ron, particularly in the areas of technique and tactical usage. So prior to doing the *Method II* evaluation Don had to complete the *Technique Breakdown Worksheets* and a *Level Three Evaluation* (quality of techniques and tactical usage explained in the next chapter).

The major difference between the two examples shows up in the technique and tactics usage section under question two. Notice how specific numbers and percentages illustrate what happened during the fight. You can see who attacked more (Ron attacked thirteen times more than Don). You can also see who used foot combinations more effectively (Don threw seven foot combinations and scored with two.). Since there are more statistics to work with in the second method, you can make more accurate generalizations about the fight as a whole.

Notice also that the answers to the rest of the questions in this example contain statistical information. Don't ever forget to pay attention to the mental aspects of the fight.

Conclusion

Whether you choose to do a simple analysis of a particular fight (Method I) or a very detailed analysis (Method II), sometimes it's important to know the reasons why you won or lost a fight. What you find will help you train for future fights and can also put your mind at ease after a very emotional fight.

Discipline = Consistent actions and behaviors based upon principles that are rooted in goals.

Chapter Six

Level Three Evaluation

"You must have the courage to do, and the common sense to flow......."

Pendekar Paul De Thouars

Technique Quality & Tactical Use

This third level of evaluation shows you how to scrutinize two very important areas of fighting; the quality of your techniques and your ability to use fighting tactics. The "quality" of fighting techniques are analyzed for technical proficiency meaning you're looking to see if techniques are thrown correctly, and at their related attributes (speed, power, timing, etc.). Fighting "tactics," explain how techniques are used, referring to a fighter's ability to do such things as faking the opponent or drawing the opponent in, etc.

This level of evaluation like *Level Two* doesn't entirely rely on the numbers generated from the worksheets and database. You must use your observational powers to make judgments about certain aspects of fighting that aren't easy to identify such as speed and power and the use of tactics. Doing a successful evaluation at this level relies on your ability to know what a correct technique looks like and to recognize an effective approach (tactics) to landing techniques or defending against attacks. Having the ability to complete a *Level Three Evaluation* is critical to helping you meet your potential as a fighter.

Some of the most important questions addressed by this level of evaluation are as follows:

- ◆ Is the technique "technically" correct (why or why not)?
- ◆ How or when do you use it (or why)?
- ◆ How are your opponent's reacting to your techniques?
- ◆ What attributes do your techniques lack (speed, power, timing, etc.)?
- ◆ What positive attributes do your techniques possess?
- ◆ Can you use fighting tactics successfully (why or why not)?

Don't forget that each time you look at a certain element of fighting you're examining that element's contribution to your overall effectiveness as a fighter. An effective fighter wins more often than he loses. Effectiveness is a matter of achieving objectives. You can't achieve much of anything in fighting without having good techniques and strong tactical abilities in order to land the techniques.

Understanding Attributes

Before you can perform a *Level Three Evaluation,* you need to understand what "attributes" are and how they relate to fighting.

Attributes are those things that describe the motion of a technique such as speed and power. The science of physics has precise ways of determining such things as power (power equals speed times mass). The A.Y.F.M. isn't based on strict scientific procedures; it relies on your observational power and understanding of fighting to be effective. When the term "attributes" is applied to fighting it has to do with all those things which describe the motion of a technique including but not limited to:

Attributes	Explanation
1. **Speed**	The time it takes a technique to land.
2. **Power**	Impact (damage) that a technique inflicts.
3. **Timing**	The ability to judge distance, use of speed, power and mobility to land an effective technique.
4. **Mobility**	Ability to efficiently bridge the distance between you and the opponent to land a technique, a combination of techniques, or the ability to avoid getting hit – footwork.
5. **Precision**	Ability to see a target while fighting and hit it accurately.
6. **Endurance**	Ability to perform without becoming tired – conditioning.
7. **Focus**	Ability to concentrate on a goal or objective.
8. **Recovery**	Ability to retract a technique quickly and efficiently in order to mount another attack, defense, or to move.

The effectiveness of your attributes is a combination of natural skill and training. As you view your abilities on tape, you'll evaluate the effectiveness of the attributes that you excel in and those that you're lacking in.

There are also three more very important attributes that you must be aware of as you view the technical correctness of your techniques including, balance, joint placement, and telegraphing. These three attributes, more than any other, directly explain a "correct" technique. A technique could be fast and powerful, but without proper balance and joint position, it's not a correct technique. Moreover, if you're telegraphing techniques (showing the opponent what you're throwing before you throw it) you won't be able to land many techniques. Remember, a movement becomes a technique after it has a repeatable pattern, a purpose, and a name. Once this criteria is met, than there is a correct and incorrect way to throw a technique. Every technique must be thrown with balance, proper joint placement and be non-telegraphic.

Here's what to look for while evaluating your balance, joint placement, and telegraphing:

Technique Quality	Explanation
Balance	Are you able to throw the technique with good control of your hips and with a comfortable stance allowing you to throw more than one technique? Do your techniques have a good recovery? Do you maintain proper body alignment allowing you to attack, defend, and move with proper execution? Pay attention to your defensive posture – do you lean back while trying to defend yourself (which may hinder your movement), does your guard drop as the fight progresses (opening you up for attack)? Do you lean forward during your attack (which may hinder your recovery or ability to adapt to your opponent)? Etc.

Joint Placement	Are you able to position your feet and hips in the proper location in order to throw the technique correctly? Do you have the proper lines of execution? In other words, does your leg during a front kick stay forward or does it look more like a bad side kick? Is your striking hand in the correct position as it hits the opponent? Etc.
Telegraphing	Are you able to throw techniques without signaling to your opponent what you intend to do. Are your techniques launched without doing such things as: dropping your hands, dipping your shoulders, turning your hips, or changing your foot positions? Etc.

Here's a more extensive explanation of what to look for when evaluating attributes:

Speed: Any aspect of fighting has a speed element to it; initiation speed, footwork speed, counter speed, etc. Be prudent in your evaluation of speed, concentrate on your initiation, counter, and timing speed:

Initiation Speed - Can you make direct hits or does the opponent get away or easily block you? Can you use indirect attacks (faking, drawing, etc.) and "explode" or initiate the hit effectively?

Counter Speed - Can you see a counter to the opponent's attack or defense and successfully hit him?

Timing Speed - Can you successfully adjust to the pace of the fight in order to match the opponent's speed, go faster than the opponent, or if you can't keep up with the opponent, can you use other tactics in order to score?

Power: Can your techniques either hurt the opponent or affect the opponent's balance? Don't just look at the power of your punches and kicks, but also look at the use of power in your defensive tactics – blocks, parries, grabs, etc., they all have a power element to them.

Mobility: One of the most important aspects of fighting! Without exceptional footwork, you'll be a very limited fighter. Maintain your ability to move and to launch techniques at any time in the fight! Look for anything that prevents you from scoring or making an effective defensive counter. Such things could include; excessive leaning backwards or to the side, being forced into a strictly defensive posture, loss of balance, or when you end up standing on one foot.

Timing: Can you recognize what is happening in the fight and respond appropriately? Timing is a combination of technique choice, distance, mobility, and precision. Examine how all these aspects work together in your fighting.

Precision: Can you hit what you see when you want to hit it? Make sure you're picking appropriate techniques for the situation. For example, you won't want to throw a spinning kick if the opponent is too close to you.

Endurance: Examine what happens to your fighting ability when you become tired. Plan your training around those aspects that you identify. In other words, if your defense is the first thing to go as you become tired, than pay attention to that in your training.

Focus: When your mind fails so does your body. Are you able to stay on task throughout the fight no matter what happens – no matter what adjustments you have to make? Put aside all self-defeating emotions such as fear, doubt, and anger. When do you become "off-track" or "unfocused?"

Recovery: Good recovery is important to your ability to transition from one technique to the next, or from an offensive movement to a defensive movement and visa-versa. Are you able to flow from one technique to another with good form? Fight with the sense that techniques don't have an ending – they always lead to something else. Be able to flow from one attack to another, from attacking to defending, and from defending to attacking with as little break in your rhythm as possible.

Understanding Tactics

Fighting tactics are maneuvers needed to gain an advantage or "edge" over an opponent to help secure victory. Tactics describe the use of techniques, such as faking high and hitting low. A tactic is different from a strategy. A strategy is a plan of action make up of one or more tactics. In other words, tactics are the ingredients that make a strategy. Chapter ten explains strategy and tactics in detail, along with how to create complete strategies. Right now, at this level of evaluation, it's important to be able to recognize which tactics you use and to judge whether or not they're effective.

Common Tactical Mistakes To Look For

♦ Don't really use tactics beyond just doing such things as increasing speed or level of aggression, etc.

♦ Over using a certain tactic, such as shifting weight on the back leg and trying to wait for the opponent.

♦ Mind goes "blank" and the fighter is unable to really do anything beyond pure reaction
or freezing up.

♦ Use the wrong tactic against the opponent, like trying to "out speed" a very fast opponent, or trying to punch threw someone who has good defensive hand skills.

♦ Trying to use a tactic for which you don't have the skill to do, such as using unconvincing fakes.

♦ Trying to use the same tactic over and over again even though it doesn't work (can't adapt).

Understanding The "Atomic" Structure Of Fighting

Every technique has a history made up of the following; what happened before the technique started, what happened during the flight of the technique, the result of the technique, and what happened after the technique landed or missed.

Techniques also have an associated intention carried out by some sort of tactic. In other words, the fighter's intention could be to hit the opponent's stomach with a reverse punch. The tactic used to land the punch could be a high fake to distract the opponent's attention away from his stomach.

So intention governs fighting, for intention will always determine which tactic you're going to use, which in turn will determine the type of technique or combination of techniques you'll employ.

This is the "atomic" structure of fighting – the most fundamental "make-up" of fighting. Here are two examples of the fundamental structure of fighting:

Example #1:

You want to land a side kick to the stomach by faking a high backfist to draw the opponent's attention up.

<u>Intention</u> = land a side kick to the stomach.

<u>Tactic(s)</u> = fake high to draw the opponent's attention away from his stomach area.

<u>Techniques</u> = high backfist, side kick.

Example #2:

You want to make a direct attack to the opponent using the following combination, front punch, reverse punch, angle to the side and side kick.

<u>Intention</u> = land a combination of techniques.

<u>Tactic(s)</u> = direct attack, angular attack.

<u>Techniques</u> = front punch, reverse punch, side kick.

These two examples show fighting is made up of a set of exchanges between opponents. Each exchange has an intention, tactic(s), and technique(s) with the ultimate goal of defeating the opponent. The *Level Three Evaluation Worksheet* examines the "atomic" structure of your fighting.

How To Perform A Level Three Evaluation

To do a *Level Three Evaluation* correctly you need to have a good understanding of how the techniques you throw are supposed to look. You must be able to judge whether or not the techniques are effective and to explain why they are or are not effective. Your knowledge of techniques must also be collaborated with your knowledge of fighting tactics.

Here are the general steps that you should follow to perform a technical and fighting tactic evaluation:

4. Review your technique breakdown worksheets and personal fighting database.

2. Pick one or more techniques, movements, attributes, or fighting principles, which you want to evaluate or improve on.

3. View your fights on video and complete the *Technical & Tactical Evaluation Worksheet* by answering all the questions.

4. Design workouts to correct the problems you find and/or to enhance the skills you already have.

Completing The Level Three Worksheet

The *Level Three Worksheet* (Technical & Tactical Evaluation) consists of five probing questions. To answer the questions, draw from all of your knowledge about fighting along with what you observe from the videotapes. First, you need to pick what you want to evaluate. If you pick a technique than evaluate the technique's technical aspects, associated attributes, and how you use them tactically. Or, you can examine attributes or tactic usage by themselves, such as looking at your hand speed, or at the effectiveness of your defense. You may want to combine different elements such as studying how your footwork affects your roundhouse kicks. The possibilities for comparison are endless and so are your opportunities to improve.

Examine the following examples to see how to make the best use of the *Level Three Worksheet*.

Technique Quality & Tactical Use: *Example One*

Technical & Tactical Evaluation
Level Three Evaluation

Name: *Kevin Murphy* Date: *2/10/97*

Tape # *7* Counter # *0-1450* Analysis # (s) *9-19*

1. This evaluation is based on how many fights? *11*

2. What are you evaluating or comparing? *Technical quality of my backfist.*

3. Is it technically correct? Why or why not? *Sometimes it's telegraphed. My backfist only has a 23% scoring percentage. Penetration is off. I miss too often. Footwork and reaction time need to improve.*

4. What are the strong points and weak points in the following attributes of what you are evaluationg?

Speed: *Good - but want to increase it!*

Power: *Need more penetration and better impact*

Timing: *Needs improvement*

Mobility: *Needs improvement - opponent's are moving out of the way*

Precision: *Good*

Endurance: *Good*

Focus: *Need more confidence in my backfist*

Recovery: *Good*

5. What tactics do you use to land these techniques and are they effective? Why or why not?

Hand and foot fakes - not always effective, want to make them more convincing. Use the backfist to set up reverse punch and side kick. Trap and use a counter backfist - this is where I need penetration to score before the opponent moves.

Notes:

I'll analyze how my footwork is affecting my backfist next. It seems that most of my problems scoring with the backfist are related to my footwork and timing.

This fighter decides to take a critical look at his backfist. He discovers that his low scoring percentage with the backfist is the result of a combination of slow footwork and bad timing. Tactically, he finds there are times when his fakes aren't very effective in setting the opponent up to land the backfist, and he also tends to telegraph the backfist.

In the notes section he decides to do the evaluation again but this time look more carefully at how his footwork affects the use of his backfist.

Technique Quality & Tactical Use: *Example Two*

Technique Quality & Tactical Use: *Example Two*

Technical & Tactical Evaluation
Level Three Evaluation

Name: *Kevin Murphy* Date: *2/10/97*

Tape # *7* Counter # *1450* Analysis # (s) *9-19*

1. This evaluation is based on how many fights? *11*

2. What are you evaluating or comparing? *Backfist and footwork - how my footwork affects the use of my backfist.*

3. Is it technically correct? Why or why not? *There's a problem with the timing of my backfist and the use of penetrating footwork. My backfist has a scoring percentage of 23%.*

4. What are the strong points and weak points in the following attributes of what you are evaluationg?

Speed: *Backfist speed is good - need to increase footwork speed*

Power: *Backfist needs for penetration and impact - increase leg strength*

Timing: *Timing between footwork and backfist needs improvement*

Mobility: *Opponent's are moving out of the way, need better explosion in my footwork*

Precision: *Good*

Endurance: *Good*

Focus: *Need more confidence in my footwork and backfist, better anticipation*

Recovery: *Good*

5. What tactics do you use to land these techniques and are they effective? Why or why not?

My backfist isn't very effective because of a lack of penetration and good timing with my footwork. Need to develop more methods to apply the backfist such as drawing the opponent in, moving side to side, counter backfist, and exploding footwork.

Notes:

I will use the above information to plan workouts designed to increase the efficiency of my footwork and timing. I will also develop my "tactics" or different ways to use the backfist.

This evaluation looks at the effect that footwork has on his backfist. This fighter is concerned that his backfist misses more often than it scores. He's not able to use penetrating footwork to get close enough to the opponent to increase his chances of scoring. He also sees weaknesses in his timing and footwork.

He uses the notes section to outline what he wants to do next. He's going to focus his training on improving his mobility and wants to find more ways to use the backfist tactically.

Conclusion

It's always beneficial to have someone else's help you evaluate your performance on any level, especially if it's someone who's knowledgeable and cares enough to be honest with you. This is especially true for this third level of evaluation where you're making critical judgments about the quality of your techniques and how you use tactics. You can't utilize new techniques and tactics until the ones you know currently are at a certain level of efficiency (meaning you can score with them on a consistent basis). As you add new skills constantly evaluate their effectiveness. <u>Define efficiency as anything that helps you score more easily</u>. Techniques that have proper execution, have strong attributes, and demonstrate good planning (tactics), are the techniques of successful fighters.

*Author **Darin Waugh***

Chapter Seven

Level Four Evaluation

"If a fighter hasn't tested his skills against an opponent he's limited in his ability to adapt to what his opponent will do."

Ricardo Wilson

Comparing Your Fighting Ability To Others

Do you want to be like the best? What makes the champion stand out or the master so spectacular? Is he born with it? Is it that elusive "star" quality, or a gift from God? Is excellence simply a matter of hard work and dedication? The same methods that you use to find what your true abilities are can also be used to discover the unique skills of those fighters you want to emulate. Discovering how other fighters use techniques and tactics allows you to compare your abilities to theirs. You'll not only gain extraordinary insight into what makes the "best" so different from the rest, but will understand what's required of you to "mirror" those whom you admire.

So far in this book you've learned how to collect statistics from a number of fights and to examine how the numbers changed over time. You've learned how to determine why you won or lost a particular fight, and to detect any flaws in your technical abilities. Unlike the first three levels of evaluation in which you focused on your own performance and your reactions to what the opponent did, the fourth level of evaluation will show you how to compare yourself to other fighters.

There are two types of comparative analyses that you can conduct. You can either compare yourself to others of your same level of experience, or to martial artists who are better than you. "Better than you," as it applies here, is someone who can outscore you (or defeat you) more often than you can outscore him. Comparing yourself to fighters of lesser skill obviously doesn't make much sense.

Completing a fighter comparison involves two basic steps. First, create a performance profile of the fighter you're being compared to, and secondly, contrast that fighter's ability with your own.

The following is a partial list of what you'll gain by comparing and contrasting yourself to other fighters:

1. Increased ability to see and interpret what other fighters do.
2. Help you clearly know and understand what is "good" or "advanced."
3. Gain a true reflection of other fighter's skills in such areas as:

   A. Technique usage patterns.
   B. Scoring percentages.
   C. Which attributes contribute most to other fighters success.
   D. The use of tactics and strategy.
   E. Probable emphasis of other fighters training.

4. Differences in styles.
5. Differences in types of fighters.

Who To Compare Yourself To

There are six different categories of fighters that you should consider comparing yourself to:

1. The standard of excellence (the champion).
2. Fighters better than you of your same style.
3. Fighters better than you of different styles.
4. A sample of fighters of mixed styles.
5. Fighters of your same rank and same style.
6. Fighters of your same rank of different styles.

Each one of these categories offers you a unique perspective on how you perform in relationship to other martial artists.

The Standard Of Excellence

The ideal person to compare yourself to is the fighter who defines the standard of excellence for your sport -- the one who has risen to the top, above all others, the champion! Developing a profile of the "standard of excellence" allows you to gain knowledge like no other method besides actually training directly with the champion. Since most martial artists don't have direct access to "champions," this level of evaluation gives you a method that allows you to contrast your skills with that of the "standard." Possessing detailed information about the fighter or fighters you admire provides a rich set of ideas for you to use in planning your workouts.

Champions achieve success because they're either specialists, have certain advanced attributes, or a combination of both. For example, a specialist in kicking may have an increased chance of winning by virtue of being a fantastic kicker. Seventy percent of his scoring techniques may be with kicks. Or, a fighter may have a certain attribute that makes him difficult to beat, such as speed. Some fighters may be able to combine good kicks with speed. Champions are also well trained, are experienced (meaning they know how the game is played), and know how to use tactics.

Should you develop specialty techniques, attributes, and tactics? If you're already scoring 50% of your points with kicks, will increasing your ability to score with kicks to 70% be a practical option for you? Remember, the goal of studying other fighters is to help you discover your own standard of excellence. A part of achieving excellence should include a "specialty" technique and attribute -- plus the ability to use them with tactics and strategy. If you aren't sure what your specialties are, or should be, the A.Y.F.M. will point them out as you analyze your fights.

Be diligent in your study of champions. They're already doing what you want to achieve.

> ### Define your own standard of excellence!

Comparisons With Your Own Style

Whereas the champion may determine the standard of excellence in a particular form of fighting, you may not feel that this person qualifies as the "standard" for you. Perhaps you want to emulate someone who fights the same way you do or has your same body type. Or, you may want to study someone of higher rank in your own style. Doing a comparison with someone of your same style is easier to do because you're already familiar with the techniques and tactics that style employs.

By studying the numbers produced (such as those logged on the fighting database), and what types of techniques are used in what proportions by those of higher rank in your system, you'll see the likely future of your own performance. That is, unless you choose to take a different course of training than your classmates, you'll probably fight like them and produce similar performance numbers.

Therefore, those who are good in a particular style are experts in the style's emphasis of combat. For example, if the style emphasizes circular techniques than you're apt to find the better practitioners scoring with more techniques that use circular motions. Still, each practitioner adds his own flavor to the system. It's this "flavor," or how someone may use angles a little differently, that sets him apart from other practitioners in his system. Developing your own "flavor" should be a priority in your course of study.

It's a great challenge to compete with those of higher levels in your own art, but the greater challenge occurs when you compete with martial artists from different styles.

Comparisons With Different Styles

Examining other styles of martial arts in contrast to your own is an extremely valuable exercise. Many martial artists aren't willing to look beyond their own system to see that there is more than one way to approach fighting. This is unfortunate, because understanding other styles gives you information about what to expect if you ever compete or spar against someone of another style. You may also learn something that you can put in your arsenal *(In chapter twelve on becoming a superior fighter it's recommended that you develop a "change-up" or a specialty technique. This technique could come from another art.)*. If you don't expose yourself to other arts, you're limiting your experience and knowledge about fighting.

How To Perform A Fighter Comparison

The same breakdown worksheets and evaluation worksheets that you use to analyze your own abilities are also used to complete a fighter comparison. Depending on what you want to know about the fighter you're investigating, you can choose to do any level of breakdown or evaluation. Obviously, if you do a complete analysis (the first three levels) you'll achieve a more complete picture of the fighter you're examining.

As indicated earlier in the chapter, you first have to videotape or obtain videotaped fights of the fighter you want to create a profile of and then choose which breakdowns or evaluations that you want to do. For example, if you want to examine how your scoring percentage compares with another fighter, use the technique breakdown sheets to find the fighter's scoring percentage. Then place both your scoring percentage and the other fighters scoring percentage together on the *Fighter Comparison Worksheet*.

The *Fighter Comparison Worksheet* lists the most important factors for you to consider in your comparison. If the worksheet doesn't contain what you want to compare then add it to the worksheet or create your own worksheets.

The following is a summary of the steps involved in creating a comparison profile:

1. Video someone with more skill than yourself or someone of the same rank or level (at least three fights if possible).

2. Use the worksheet(s) that will log the information you need to do the comparison (from any one or all of the levels of evaluation).

3. Compare your performance with that of the person you've created a profile of by completing the *Fighter Comparison Worksheet*.

4. Develop training routines so that you can acquire the same kind of skill as the person you've chosen, or use the information to develop strategies to defeat those who are of your same rank.

5. Define your own standard of excellence.

Some Key Points To Keep In Mind

Pick three of your most recent fights in which you did well, or...

♦ Try to compare like performances, in other words, if you use three fights in which you performed well use three fights in which the other fighter performed well also. If you compare poor performances or even a mixture of poor and good performances, be sure to make note of it.

♦ Do your best to acquire at least three videotaped fights of the person you're making a comparison of. While having only one or two fights recorded will certainly give you a tremendous amount of information to work with, having as many fights as possible to break down and evaluate leads to more accurate and reliable comparisons.

♦ Some types of tournaments may not allow for much individual style differences because of the rules, always remember that tournament fighting is "limiting" and may not allow a fighter to utilize his full capacity of skills.

♦ Fighters at the same level as you may lack the necessary ability to take full advantage of your weaknesses. Sparring someone of your same level often becomes a game of wit based on some small advantage. Sparing someone with great skill forces you to exist in the arena of cunning and experience. Go there as often as possible.

If you're lucky enough to have a videotape of you fighting someone far superior than yourself, surely you would want to study the video very meticulously and use all the levels of evaluation outlined in the A.Y.F.M. You'll see many weaknesses in your abilities as you fight someone of greater skill, but you should also see potential. The potential for your uniqueness as a fighter to one day possess the skills of a superior fighter.

Don't be afraid to interview the person you sparred with after the sparring session is over. Ask what he feels your strengths and weaknesses are. Ask how he's able to score against you. Get his training ideas on how you can improve. Keep all this information as part of your notes and incorporate that information into your training. Maybe you could even persuade this person to sit down and watch the videotape with you.

♦ Sometimes you can't be sure whether or not the other fighter has an injury or if there are other factors affecting his performance, unless you have the opportunity to ask him. Actually, it's rather safe to say that it's very difficult for anyone to perform at his extreme best all the time. It's difficult to judge the mental outlook of fighters -- emotions can create surprising results.

♦ Since there's such a variety of martial arts styles and because everyone differs in body type, motivation, likes and dislikes, etc., your comparisons can never be totally accurate. Make speculations based on facts not guesses, and keep good notes.

♦ As you're analyzing the performance of a fighter with greater skill than you, keep in mind the level of his opponent's skill. More than likely his opponent's skill is above yours as well. So keep track of how the fighter you're analyzing handles different opponents.

♦ There's no "ultimate" example or pattern for martial artists to follow. There are many examples for you to emulate and study from, but you must decide the "example" you'll become. As stated above, define your own standard of excellence!

Important Message About Training

In studying fighters you see the results of training. Having information about how other fighters train is just as important as breaking down and understanding performance. Training is always based on expected results -- a fighter's performance is the result of the training that preceded it. To understand what makes someone skillful, you have to know how he trains. If the opportunity is available to you, train with the person or people you admire or go and watch them workout.

Make yourself familiar with how other styles train. What is the emphasis of their training? What makes that style different? What skills does a fighter from that style likely to possess? What training methods does that style use?

How To Complete The Fighter Comparison Worksheet

The *Fighter Comparison Worksheet* is very similar to the *Personal Fighting Database*, with a few modifications. The main difference is that the *Fighter Comparison Worksheet* accommodates information about two different fighters. This way you can easily compare the results of your analysis because all the vital information is right beside each other. The other difference between the database and the worksheets is the addition of more information about the fighter's attributes, use of strategy, pace, distance, etc.

Review and examine the following example of a *Fighter Comparison Data Worksheet* before you attempt to complete one.

Fighter Comparison Worksheet
Level Four Evaluation

Reason(s) You Are Using This Fighter For Comparison: *He's the current state champion*

Fighter's Names:	1. *Daniel McConnell*	2. *Matt Bennett*
Number Of Fights Analyzed For Comparison?	3	3
Scoring % Kicks & Punches:	31 %	39 %
Scoring % Kicks:	67 %	79 %
Scoring % Hands:	33 %	21 %
Total Punches Thrown:	471	325
Total Kicks Thrown?	104	187
Movement: (Attacks & Defenses)	135 Attacks 72 Defends	90 Attacks 125 Defends
Combinations:	66	82
Most Commonly Used Offensive Tactic?	Hand and foot fakes followed by roundhouse kicks	Uses good movement, keeps his distance and picks his shots
Most Commonly Used Defensive Tactic:	Slip inside and upper cut	Counter punching
Attributes: Strengths	Good focus. Powerful inside punches	Good conditioning, strong build. Good mobility - good timing
Attributes: Weaknesses	- Timing not all that good (wild) - Clumsy footwork - Poor technique in general	- Not very powerful - looses control at times - Doesn't area well w/ kicks
Explain Fighters Use Of Tactics & Strategy.	Likes to throw hand and foot fakes and then try to get inside and slug it out. Never moves back	Likes to use stop hit and counter punching. Move and hit.
How Does The Fighter Use Distance?	Aggressively attacks and never backs up	Likes to move and hit and counter punch
How Does The Fighter Use Pace?	Very aggressive constantly attacks	Tries to counter punch and move out of the way
What Areas Of Fighting Does The Fighter Specialize In?	Aggressive slugger	Move and hit - counter puncher
Emphasis Of Training? (Stlye, Etc.)	Heavy bag, road work, sparring, Kickboxing	Movement drills, focus gloves, jump rope, etc. Kickboxing

General Conclusions (Training Ideas, Etc.): *Our styles are totally different. He likes to move and counter punch. I like to be aggressive and attack. To beat him I'll have to learn how to contain him and force him to fight on the inside. I'll need to increase my over all skill, training, confidence, etc. I'm going to seek out training partners to spar who fights like he does.*

In the above example, Daniel finds that Matt has a totally different approach to kick-boxing than he does. He admires Matt's ability to move and counter punch, how he maintains his distance to "pick his shots," and how he uses stop hits. Matt has become state champion by using these tactics to form a very successful strategy.

Dan has noted not only tactics he thinks he can use against Matt, but also wants to develop some of Matt's abilities. Daniel realizes that he has been winning on his aggressiveness and that his skill level in technique usage and footwork need to improve before he can hope to become state champion and move on to becoming a world class champion.

Interpreting The Results

The main goal of the comparison is to discover what makes other fighters more skilled than you -- giving you insight on how to become a better fighter. As you examine the *Comparison Worksheet*, notice the big differences in numbers first. Does he throw more techniques than you do, and by what percentage? Is he able to use combinations more effectively than you, etc.? As you go through each category on the *Fighter Comparison Worksheet* you should do the following:

1. Make judgments about how each category contributes to your success and the success of the other fighter.

2. You can also combine categories to create a more in-depth profile of the other fighter and yourself.

A. Is he good because of superior technique usage combined with a certain attribute?
B. Is he a good tactician in using kicks?
C. Does he combine a great sense of distance and timing?
D. Etc.

Conclusion

The results of a fighter comparison are often surprising and unexpected! A better fighter than you may actually have a lower scoring percentage -- meaning he throws a lot of techniques without scoring very often. He may be a risky fighter and therefore not someone you want to learn anything from. You may find that he scores almost totally with kicks but throws an even amount of kicks and punches. Obviously, there are more ways than one to win, and understanding as many of these strategies as possible will greatly increase your knowledge of fighting. The more ways you can discover to win and utilize the better!

Chapter Eight

Level Five Evaluation

"Attitude is by far the most important aspect in martial arts."

Joe Lewis

Thinking Like A Fighter

This evaluation is about the battle you wage within yourself to control your emotions, to maintain your confidence, and to stay disciplined in your action. The conflict with your emotions is as much of a struggle, if not more of a struggle, than facing an opponent. Your mind is your greatest weapon. It alone can determine if you win or loss. Your physical expression is a direct result of your mental attitude. No evaluation of fighting would be complete without examining how your mind affects your performance.

If you're scared, than your techniques and tactics will reflect your fears. Fear can cause you to be apprehensive and/or too over react. Tactics are successful when you're confident and focused. Fighting starts in the mind. Thoughts and emotions that sort through options toward an expected result precede actions.

As you plan the results of your techniques (scoring) from all your options (tactics), always attach a positive emotion to your actions (confidence, focus, etc.). In order to do this, you must first understand how your thought process works as you fight.

Knowing how your thoughts, emotions, and attitude affect your performance is paramount to discovering how you can improve in any aspect of fighting. Every technique you throw has an emotional component to it. To know that emotional component is to recall how your thoughts, emotions, and reactions produced your fighting performance. Your fighting performance is not a result of what you did. It's a result of what you thought and felt.

This fifth level of evaluation will show you how to recognize your thinking and emotional patterns as you fight. This is done by recalling and logging your thoughts and emotions during each of the following parts of a fight:

1. Before each exchange of techniques (whether it's an attack or a defense).
2. During each exchange of techniques.
3. After each exchange of techniques.

Each part in an exchange of techniques, before, during, and after is explained in more detail in the section on how to complete the *Retrospection Worksheet*.

In addition to discovering your dominant tactical and emotional patterns while fighting you'll also explore how your thinking affects your performance in these aspects of fighting as well:

1. How you responded to your performance right after the fight.
2. How you responded to the environment in which you fought in.
3. How efficiently you mentally prepared yourself during the day of the fight.
4. How efficiently you mentally prepared yourself during training.
5. What your body language tells your opponents and how it affects your overall performance.
6. How you responded to watching the videotape of your performance.

How To Do A Retrospective Evaluation

The mental evaluation uses observational recall or "retrospection," meaning that as you view the fight you'll need to recall your thoughts and feelings as you fought. The emphasis of the analysis is on what you were thinking or feeling and not on what you did (in terms of techniques). If you felt angry, you'll record that you felt angry. If a certain tactic came to mind like faking low and hitting high, you would write that down.

You might find that you become frustrated very easily, or that you can't really organize your thoughts and reactions in any congruent manner. Maybe you'll discover in yourself such admirable qualities as the ability to concentrate, to calmly react to change, and accept winning and defeat with honor. To find out, each attack and defense is broken into three phases; before the action (or before any techniques are thrown), during the action (when a defensive or offensive technique is used), and after the exchange of techniques (when the fighters get ready for the next attack or defense). This leaves you with a list of thoughts, emotions, and reactions that will allow you to make general conclusions about your mental abilities. The *Retrospection Worksheet* catalogues your thoughts, emotions, and reactions according to the three phases of fighting.

Two of the most important conclusions that come from doing a mental evaluation is identifying your dominant tactical methodology and your dominant emotions as you fight. This determines what motivates you during a fight and what tends to frustrate you. The following section will expand your understanding of the three phases of fighting so that you can do an effective mental evaluation. After you understand the three phases of fighting, you're ready to complete the *Retrospection Worksheet*.

The Three Phases Of Fighting

To complete the mental evaluation you first need to understand how each exchange of techniques between fighters can be broken down into three phases. Understanding these three phases is not only essential to completing the *Retrospection Worksheet,* but it's also important to your understanding of fighting in general, and to your strategic and tactical planning as your skill increases. Once you understand how your thoughts and emotions work in each phase of fighting, you'll develop a better feel for when to use certain tactics under certain situations.

The worksheet documents your thoughts and feelings during each phase of action.

1. Before: This is the time when you and your opponent are stalking each other, jousting for position, and trying to find the right moment to attack. This is when you may be deciding which tactic to use. Every choice of attack or defense is usually made up of an emotional and tactical component. Sometimes you may do things out of anger or desperation and choose tactics that express those emotions. Advanced fighters decide to use tactics based on reasoning and planning (if they plan ahead, before the fight, this is considered a strategy). Advanced fighters also use reaction and adaptation more easily. Responses that occur with no emotion or pre-determined tactic are a result of a state of mind often referred to as "no-mind." In other words, "no-mind" is a response that has no thinking -- just reaction as if it had no mind. Advanced fighters are able to use both a clear thinking process (to fight tactically) and pure response (which allows them to respond quickly and correctly to change). It should be one of your goals to have "no-mind" as one of your fighting tactics.

2. During: This is the time when you're either attacking or defending -- when the actual exchange of techniques is taking place; you have either attacked or are defending yourself with the benefit of a tactic, or with no tactic in mind. If you don't have a tactic in mind during an exchange of techniques, than you're either responding out of pure reaction or from some emotion such as fear or anger, as explained above. This is the time when you may have to change tactics or techniques to adapt to the situation at hand. For example, you may have tried to fake with a low kick intending to hit high, but the opponent doesn't fall for the fake and throws a spinning kick --

you must respond by abandoning your initial set-up (the low kick) and change tactics in order to stop the spin kick and to land a counter move.

3. After: This is the time when an exchange of techniques has ended. In a point karate tournament, this occurs when there is a score, a possible score, or when someone goes out of bounds (the referee controls when fighters can or cannot fight). In boxing, the time between exchanges is shorter, and is more often controlled by the fighters (or the rhythm of the fight), which leaves less time to think of new tactics. The "after" phase is when you evaluate what just happened and begin to think of a new tactic. Once you have your next tactic in mind and/or you and the opponent begin stalking each other again, you enter back into the "before" stage.

During the three phases of fighting the intensity of the action goes from looking each other over to the engagement of techniques until there is a break in the action. Just as the physical interaction between fighters starts with a low intensity and increases as the fight continues, the emotional attachment begins low and increases as the fight goes on too. Each fighter will test the other fighter's emotional fortitude to see at what state (or level) of emotional control he's at. The advanced fighter knows that it's much more important to defeat the opponent's mind than it is to beat his body!

Emotional Response & Pure Reaction

Evaluating your thinking and emotions as you fight involves not only understanding the three phases of fighting but also knowing the difference between an "emotional response" and "pure reaction."

Emotional Response: An emotional response is a sudden change in your emotional state like going from calm to fear or from fear to rage. If your emotions are out of control, your ability to fight well is too! If you can't deal with your own emotions than you may end up being frozen and unable to fight at all, or even worse, you may try to intentionally hurt your opponent. An emotional response is something that can occur at any time during a fight. Carefully note emotional responses in your evaluation.

Pure Reaction: A "pure reaction" is something that you do "tactically," either attacking or defending, without thinking about it first. Normally, while fighting you can plan or think about what tactic you want to do. For example, you may decide to counter the opponent's next kick with a flying backfist. So when the opponent kicks, you blast him with a flying backfist. This wouldn't be a pure reaction because you planned ahead. If you had just reacted to the opponent's kick with a flying backfist without planning, than this is considered a "pure reaction." Fighters must rely on their reactions to save them from defeat at many moments during a fight. The ability to think and use tactics while at the same time allowing the mind and body to purely react to change is one of the greatest challenges to becoming a superior fighter. Often in the martial arts, the ability to react without thought is called "no-mind" -- fighting with pure reaction as if no mind is controlling it.

The following is a summary of the three phases of fighting, plus the definitions for "emotional response" and "pure reaction."

The Phases Of Fighting

1. **Before**	Stalking the opponent, thinking of a technique and tactic to use.
2. **During**	The exchange of techniques, when you use the tactic you thought of or switch to another tactic in order to adapt to change.
3. **After**	When you evaluate what happened and look for another tactic.
4. **Emotional Response**	Sudden change in emotional state (you suddenly become angry, frustrated, happy, etc.) can happen at any time during a fight,
5. **Pure Reaction**	You do something without thinking, sometimes referred to as "no-mind."

Tactics Versus The Setup

Be sure to know the distinction between a tactic and setting the opponent up. "Tactics" are what you use to "setup" the opponent for some outcome, usually in order to score. There can also be other types of tactics designed for other purposes such as stalling for time or to keep from getting injured (like covering up after you were hit), etc. In any case, you're attempting to secure a certain outcome by setting-up the opponent to fail in his tactics by executing your tactics with greater skill, tactfulness, or deceit. This is the nature of fighting and without question the most important type of tactic is one that sets the opponent up for a score.

Two Rules Of Thumb In Doing A Mental Analysis:
1. **Don't exaggerate.** 2. **Don't get down on yourself.**

Completing The Retrospection Worksheet

Here are the steps involved in doing a mental evaluation of your thoughts and emotions as you fight:

Retrospection Worksheet
Level Five Evaluation Summary

Name: *Mark Caso*   Date: *11/14/96*

     Tape #: *14*   Counter #: *1020*   Analysis #: *31*

Tournament: *X*   Sparring: ____   Event: *Red Dragon Championships*

Opponent(s): *Ben Franklin*

1. Summerize your dominant feeling(s) or emotion(s) as you fight?

Before: *Anxious, nervous*

During: *Calm and focused*

After: *Start to get nervous again*

Cause: *Not able to control nervous feelings at competitions.*

2. Summerize your dominant thoughts as you fight?

Before: *Picking tactics from my strategy*

During: *Concerned with his reactions*

After: *Want to pick another tactic and quickly attack again*

Cause: *I'm aggressive*

3. Summarize your dominant tactical responses while attacking?

a. *Stay aggressive and attack*

b. *Jam opponents and use combinations*

c. *Quicken my pace and technique speed*

4. Summarize your dominant tactical responses while defending?

a. *Move and counter punch*

b. *Jam and counter punch*

c. *Increase pace to make opponent miss*

1. Make copies of the *Retrospection Worksheet* (as many as you need).

2. Review the fight on videotape.

3. Log your thoughts, feelings, and reactions according to the phase of action (before, during, and after the exchange of techniques) on the first part of the worksheet.

4. Answer the summary questions on the second part of the worksheet.

5. Interpret your results.

6. Plan your training and research based on the results.

To complete the *Retrospection Worksheet* you need to view the fight and recall what your thinking process was as you fought. As you fill in the information on the worksheet keep your comments simple -- don't worry about using complete sentences. Stay away from making assumptions, "I guess I started to get tired." Either you were or you weren't tired. Instead say, "I became tired and apprehensive." Identify your exact feelings and thoughts; never just write something down as an excuse. The evaluation is useless if you're not honest with yourself. The worst thing you can do is exaggerate. Most people when they recreate what occurred in a fight "glorify" what really happened. You can't exaggerate when you review the action from videotaped fights, but there's no way to videotape your thought process. If you exaggerate, you only hurt yourself. Being honesty with yourself is the first rule of martial arts training. To act any other way is not only egotistical but could be dangerous!

Some Key Points To Keep In Mind

♦ Remember that sometimes you just have a "pure reaction," be sure to write that down.

♦ You may not recall your thinking or emotions during each exchange so write down that you couldn't remember.

♦ It's also very common to carry the same emotion and thought process into more than one exchange.

♦ Many fighters (particularly inexperienced fighters) will use the same tactical response repeatedly even though it didn't work the first, second, or third time.

♦ Take your time and don't worry about logging each attack or defense. This is difficult to do in some forms of fighting such as boxing or kick-boxing. Be sure to pay particular attention to key periods during the fight, like when you either dominated the opponent or you had a strong emotional response such as anger, etc.

♦ Again, you may not always know what you were thinking or feeling. The most important thing for you to do is to find your dominant emotion, your dominant thinking process, and your dominant tactical philosophy. Your memory will improve as you do more retrospective analyses.

♦ Watch your facial expressions and body language. Everything that you do not only gives you information about yourself but gives your opponents information also. Learn to recognize what your body language is telling your opponents. Facial expressions and body language can communicate such things as fear, confidence, injury, determination, etc. Unless you're an experienced fighter and in control of your emotions, what you're thinking will show up on your face and in your actions.

Follow these steps on how to complete the *Retrospection Worksheet* and pay close attention to the examples:

Completing The Retrospection Worksheet

1. Complete the top portion with the following information:

Name: *Ralph Guglielmi* Date: *5/4/98*
Tape #: *4* Counter #: *150* Analysis #: *23*

Tournament: *X* Sparring: _____ Event: *Great Lake Nationals*

Opponent: *Bob Webb*

2. Start the video, carefully view each exchange of techniques, pause or stop the tape as necessary. Complete the second portion of the worksheet starting with the "before" section with your thoughts, feelings, and tactics:

Examples:

Before: (Thought or Feeling) *Nervous and anxious*
(Tactic) *Tried to maintain a comfortable distance*

Before: (Thought or Feeling) *Angry*
(Tactic) *Just tried to punch harder to hurt him*

Before: (Thought or Feeling) *Don't remember*
(Tactic) *Waited for him to attack to counter punch*

3. Complete the "during" section of the worksheet with your thoughts, feelings, and tactics:

Examples:

During: (Thought or Feeling) *Felt scared*
(Tactic) *Tried to cover up as he attacked*

During: (Thought or Feeling) *Surprised he blocked my backfist*
(Tactic) _____

During: (Thought or Feeling) *Relaxed*
(Tactic) *Changed my high roundhouse into a medium side kick*

4. Complete the "after" section of the worksheet with your thoughts, feelings, and tactics:

Examples:

After: (Thought or Feeling) *Angry he head-butted me, referee did nothing*
(Tactic) *Have to keep him from getting too close*

After: (Thought or Feeling) *Happy! I threw techniques and all scored*
(Tactic) *Keep using effective combinations*

After: (Thought or Feeling) *Twisted my ankle, made me worry*
(Tactic) *Had to resort to counter punching*

5. Answer the questions in the second section of the worksheet (explained in the next portion of this chapter on how to summarize your results). The purpose of these questions are to help you extrapolate from the first section of this worksheet your dominant fighting emotions and tactical responses.

Summarizing & Interpreting The Results

To interpret the results of the retrospective breakdown answer the summary questions on the second part of the *Retrospection Worksheet*. The second part of the worksheet contains nine important questions. These questions will show what emotions drive you and what tactics those emotions compel you to use.

Once you know the weaknesses and the strengths of your thinking, reactions, and emotions you can design training routines that will give you a clear path to becoming a confident fighter with finely tuned skill.

Also, by understanding how your mind works, you'll develop the ability to know what your opponents' are thinking also. There are common modes of thinking within all fighters.

The following is a partial list of different thinking processes you could be experiencing as you fight:

How does your thinking process work?

- Feelings come to me and I respond.
- I gather clues and I respond.
- I just try things and see what happens.
- I question myself as I fight.
- I worry too much about getting hurt.
- I rely too much on my strengths.
- I try to have no thoughts even thoughts of self.
- I'm conscience of what other people think.
- I'm very nervous, have butterflies......
- I don't like to fight.
- I become easily distracted, angry, and frustrated.
- I don't prepare myself very well mentally or physically.
- I can't seem to make my tactics work.
- Most of the time I'm calm and confident.

Obviously, this list could go on for pages, and hopefully, not all the comments about yourself are negative ones. There is no such thing as a perfect fighter. A good fighter is able to counter balance negative actions and thoughts with positive ones. A superior fighter is able to tip the balance more on the positive side and therefore consistently out scores his opponents. The following shows how a superior fighter should function in each phase of fighting:

Superior Thinking While Fighting

Before:	Confident, aware, thinking and reacting, choosing tactics from a well-planned strategy.
During:	Executes tactics with a high percentage of success and with a convincing ability to land techniques; uses a consistent defense, adapts to changes with good reactions, keeps emotions under control.
After:	Maintains a good fighting attitude and uses the information gained from the previous exchanges to go into the next exchange with more knowledge, stays with the strategy set up before the fight started.

Completing The Retrospection Summary Questions

Retrospection Worksheet
Level Five Evaluation Summary

Name: _Mark Caro_   Date: _1/14/96_
Tape #: _14_   Counter #: _1030_   Analysis #: _31_
Tournament: _X_   Sparring: _____ Event: _Red Dragon Championship_
Opponent(s): _Ben Franklin_

1. Summarize your dominant feeling(s) or emotion(s) as you fight?

Before: _Anxious, nervous_
During: _Calm and focused_
After: _Start to get nervous again_
Cause: _Not able to control nervous feelings at competitions_

2. Summarize your dominant thoughts as you fight?

Before: _Picking tactics from my strategy_
During: _Concerned with his reaction_
After: _Want to pick another tactic and quickly attack again_
Cause: _I'm aggressive_

3. Summarize your dominant tactical responses while attacking?

a. _Stay aggressive and attack_
b. _Jam opponent and use combinations_
c. _Quicken my pace and technique speed_

4. Summarize your dominant tactical responses while defending?

a. _Move and counter punch_
b. _Jam and counter punch_
c. _Increase pace to make opponent miss_

5. Summarize what your body language and facial expressions are showing?

Before: _Tend to keep my body tense showing nervousness_
During: _Tend to concentrate while defending - make various facial expressions_
After: _Tend to put my hands on my head in frustration_
Cause: _Unable to totally control my nervousness all the time_

6. Did you have any pre-fight, environmental, post-fight, etc. concerns that may have impacted your performance?

We traveled to a small town and it made me feel like an outsider. Added to my nervousness.

7. How did you prepare yourself mentally while training? Did it help you during competition? Why or why not?

My instructor had me imagine different opponents as I spar - as if I were at a tournament. It helped some because I'm not as nervous while fighting. It's between fighting and between exchanges that I'm still nervous.

8. How did you prepare yourself mentally the day of the fight? Did it help you during competition? Why or why not? _I did some breathing exercises and tried to meet some new people to make myself feel more comfortable._

9. Make a list of the areas you need to improve on?

- Need to be able to focus my nervousness
- Need to learn to be more confident
- Need to stick to my strategy and never become frustrated
- Need to keep my performance consistent

Training Ideas:
Discuss with my instructor some different mental exercises that will help me stay calm.
Make a greater effort to meet people I don't know - to build my confidence.
I'm going to study my fights on videotape and the fights of other martial artists by using the A.Y.F.M.

To complete a retrospective summary use all of the breakdown worksheets which you used to log your thinking and tactical responses during each phase of fighting. There could easily be a large number of these worksheets depending on how many attacks (exchanges to techniques) occurred in the fight.

Each question is explained in detail along with examples.

Question #1

1. Summarize your dominant feeling(s) or emotion(s) as you fight?

Before: _I have mixed emotions_

During: _It depends upon what's happening_

After: _Again, mixed feelings depending on what's happening._

Cause: _Not able to stay calm and focused - letting too many things affect me emotionally!_

Review the responses that you wrote down in the first part of the worksheet and find the expressions used most often to describe your feelings or emotions. Remember, you're after "emotional" changes in particular. An emotional change is a strong feeling, impulse, or departure from your normal mental state. If you used the words "nervous," or "apprehensive," than you can safely conclude that you generally fight while being nervous. Therefore, your "dominant" emotion while you fight is "nervousness." You could easily have more than one dominant emotion as the above example shows.

Next, determine the cause of your nervousness, anger, apprehension, or whatever it is that has an impact on how you fight. Were you nervous because of a lack of confidence or because you fought a well known competitor? Maybe, you actually fight better while being nervous. Were you angry with yourself, the opponent, or the judges? Think through each emotion from why you're having that emotion to how it's affecting your performance positively or negatively. Then determine what needs done to change your feelings and emotions to improve your ability to compete. There may be a mixture of many positive and negative factors that cause you to have emotional reactions. Most fighters seem to start with a certain degree of confidence and it changes as the fight or tournament goes on.

Some causes of strong emotional responses can include:

1. Being out of shape (as in giving up, frustration).
2. Overwhelmed by the opponent's skill.
3. Not comfortable with the environment.
4. Opponent's size (or other physical attribute).
5. Emotional distress from personal problems.
6. Strong dislike of the opponent.
7. Feeling cheated by the judges.
8. Coaches pep talk.
9. Scoring easily.
10. Difficulty scoring.
11. Losing.
12. Winning.
13. Injury.

Here is a list of some the most common emotional responses or feelings that you can have while fighting:

1. Fear.
2. Anger.
3. Nervousness (butterflies in your stomach).
4. Confidence.
5. Centered or focused.
6. Confused.
7. Worried.
8. Apprehensive.
9. Indecisive.
10. Anxious.
11. Happy.

Ideal State Of Mind While Fighting
Emotionally in control and focused on goals and strategy.

Question #2

2. Summarize your dominant thoughts as you fight?

Before: _I just want to score_

During: _I just want to score quickly_

After: _I don't stop to think – want to keep fighting_

Cause: _Just want to be aggresive – don't relax and use tactics_

To answer this question you must understand how thoughts are different from feelings. Thoughts rationalize how you feel! For example, if you're feeling scared you may be thinking, "Oh, no, I'm going to lose!" So the feeling of being "scared" is transformed into a negative thought, "to lose." And unless the "scared" feeling is turned into a positive thought, such as concentrating on scoring regardless of the fear, you'll probably lose. A positive feeling like "confidence" will generate positive thoughts such as, "I need to concentrate on my strategy." Be sure to know the difference between thoughts and feelings.

This question asks you to summarize your dominant thinking pattern(s) as you fight. Are you losing because your emotional state keeps you from showing your true ability? Or perhaps you're just unprepared mentally to handle competition? These are the kinds of conclusions you must make about how you perform. As you examine the breakdowns, separate your thoughts from your emotions.

Here is a list of common dominant thoughts and feelings that most fighters have while fighting:

Feeling	Thoughts
1. Doubt	"Oh, no, I'm losing!" "I'm going to lose!" He's too quick!" "I can't......"
2. Confidence	"I'm winning!" "I'm going to win!" "I'm ready" "I can........."
3. Confusion	"What do I do now?" "I don't understand what's going on?"
4. Questioning the situation	"What will my instructor think?" "Is everyone watching me?"
5. Focus (Concentration)	"I'm going to use what I know to the best of my ability, I'm going to land my side kick by doing..........." "My concentration is strong."
6. Unfocused	"I don't care what the guy does or who he is, I'm fighting to prove something!" "I can't seem to concentrate." "I'm not ready."
7. Preoccupation	"I hurt my ankle this week I can't fight!" "Is my girlfriend going to show up?" "He's too strong!" "I just want to look good!"

Question #3

3. Summarize your dominant tactical responses while attacking?

a. _I tend to rush the opponent with hand combinations._

b. _Use quick jerky footwork to confuse the opponent._

c. _Use a lot of hand fakes to set-up kicks._

When answering this question don't think in terms of specific techniques, but infer from the worksheets your dominant tactical choices based on your emotions and thoughts as you fought. Refer also to what you wrote in question one of this worksheet. For example, in question one you may have answered that your dominant emotional response is anger. Now write down what you do because of your anger, such as, "I become angry at opponents who taunt me, and I try to hit faster and harder." Your tactical choice "to hit harder and faster" is in response to "anger." Is this appropriate, does it achieve positive results, or do you just become "sloppy" and more ineffective? These are the kinds of questions that you have to learn to ask yourself. You must determine if you fight by emotions or by logic. Study the above examples.

Question #4

4. Summarize your dominant tactical responses while defending?

a. *I do a lot of counter punching.*

b. *Love to use the stop-kick to keep the opponent from coming in.*

c. *I can cover up well!*

Answer this question in much the same way as question number three, but instead of addressing what you do emotionally and tactically when attacking, list how you likely respond while defending.

Question #5

5. Summarize what your body language and facial expressions are showing?

Before: *Tend to keep my body tense showing nervousness*

During: *Tend to overact well defending making various facial expressions*

After: *Tend to put my hands on my head in frustration*

Cause: *Unable to control my nervousness all the time.*

Often what you're thinking or feeling shows up in your body language. This can influence how you fight and what tactical choices you make. If the opponent can indiscriminately cause you to have "emotional" reactions he can effectively control you, and the degree of control that he has on you shows up in your body language. You must learn to recognize what your body movements and facial expressions are telling the opponent.

The body language evaluation is also done in terms of the three phases of fighting. At each stage of a fight, look for "body language" that may have a negative effect on your fighting. For example, before you attack you may dip your front shoulder down in effect telegraphing when you're going to move. Anything and everything that you do conveys information about you to your opponent.

You want mental control of the fight. To achieve this, you must first have control of your own emotions no matter what happens during a fight. Don't let the opponent invoke emotional responses that distract you from fighting at your best by making you become frustrated and ineffective. The only way he knows he's getting to you "mentally" is to see it in your body language. Look confident, walk confidently, talk confidently, and never be afraid to look the opponent in the eyes. Don't allow nervousness or fear to show in your eyes, on your face, or in your demeanor. Once you have control of your own emotions, you can learn how to keep the opponent from controlling any aspect of the fight -- not the emotions, the pace of the fight, or to even let the opponent feel comfortable enough to attack or defend with full confidence. The superior fighter knows sheer dominance!

Be sure to utilize different training methods from meditation, positive thinking exercises, and continued use of the A.Y.F.M., to increase your emotional control, confidence, and discipline. Too many martial artists don't spend enough time on mental preparation. Once you have a sufficient understanding of confidence and discipline you'll no longer display body language that can be used against you.

The following chart is by no means a complete list of the different "clues" that body language can convey, but it does list some of the most common types of body language, the effect that it can have on a fighter's performance, and how it can be exploited. Study the above example and how it relates to the chart below.

Body Language	Effect	Exploited
Nervous Habits Pulling on clothing Wiping the face Cracking knuckles Looking away Fidgeting Walking around Etc.	Conveys that a fighter is nervous. Will often result in helping the other fighter feel more confident.	If one fighter can figure out why the other is nervous, he can keep the fighter nervous by doing whatever it is that keeps him uncomfortable. Or by using other antagonistic tactics.
Arm Placement On hips Back of the head Crossed over the chest	Can signal different things; fatigue, cockiness, confidence, disgust, etc.	If one fighter can figure out what the opponent is experiencing, he can exploit it. For example, if a fighter knows his opponent is tired he could constantly pressure him.
Facial Expressions Smiling, laughing, intense stare, tears, grimacing, etc.	The face can display an incredible amount of emotions. What shows up on a person's face is a result of what he is feeling and thinking. Combine facial expressions with other body language to make a better assessment.	A fighter's facial expression gives away more information about a fighter than any other form of body language. Fighters should always study their opponent's face.
Head Placement Chin on the chest Cocked to the side Looking to the ceiling Etc.	Shows such things as disgust with ones performance, the opponent, or referee; could also signal fatigue, etc.	If one fighter can figure out what the opponent is experiencing he can exploit it. For example, if a fighter is beginning to doubt himself, add to his doubt by quickly scoring on him.
Showing Pain Limping Holding the injured body part Grimacing facial expressions Crying Bending over Etc.	Any injury can immediately downgrade a fighter's ability. Fighters must discern when it's necessary to stop fighting because of injury. If a fighter continues, he must guard against the opponent exploiting his injury.	If one fighter can figure out the extent of the other fighter's injury he can continually attack that area.
Eye Contact Never looks into the opponent's eyes. Looks intently into the opponent's eyes. Looks at the opponent's shoulders or chest.	A fighter who isn't able to look his opponent in the eyes, could be nervous and fearful. A fighter who can look his opponent in the eyes is generally confident. Some fighters look at the opponent's shoulders and chest to see when he will attack.	If one fighter won't look another in the eyes he may be fearful. The other fighter should exploit his fear by dominating the fight. If the opponent is confident, the other fighter should find ways to break his concentration. If a fighter looks at the other fighter's shoulders and chest to see when he will attack, the other fighter should use shoulder and chest fakes.
Dress Fancy colored uniforms Altered uniforms No uniform Damaged uniform Etc.	If a fighter dresses radically than he is trying to bring more attention to himself.	No fighter should be worried about what another fighter is wearing. Meet the fighter's skill not his hype or ego. A damaged uniform can sometimes hinder one fighter's ability allowing the other fighter to exploit him.

| Verbal Cues
Yelling
Taunting
Talking to one's self
Etc. | Some fighters are more than willing to express what they are thinking or feeling by what they say and how they say it. Other fighters like to talk to their opponents sometimes in a teasing or taunting manner. | If a fighter expresses himself by what he says than that information can be used against him. No fighter should let another fighter's teasing or taunting affect his performance. If a fighter is affected by verbal cues it can be exploited. |

6. Did you have any pre-fight, environmental, post-fight, etc. concerns that may have impacted your performance?

This question asks you to consider if any pre-fight, environmental, or post-fight concerns had a negative effect on how you fought. Anxiety and worry before a tournament (pre-fight) can easily translate into a poor performance. There are many things that can cause you to be anxious from travel time, to a different type of tournament atmosphere (environment), to fear of disappointing your instructor or family. Sometimes, a factor such as a very disappointing loss in a previous tournament carries over into the next competition (post fight).

To answer this question consider how anything outside of the actual fight may have affected your performance either before the tournament or during the tournament.

Like every other part of this evaluation process find out what has a negative effect on your performance and then discover ways to eliminate them or turn them into something positive.

The following list gives you some things to consider as you answer this question:

Pre-Fight: *(Anytime before the tournament, from the night before to several months before.)*

- Couldn't sleep the night before.
- Long travel time.
- New and different locations.
- Extreme nervousness.
- Feeling unprepared, apprehensive, etc.
- Fear.
- Injury.
- Instructor or family expectations.
- Family tragedy.
- Personal relationship concerns.
- Job or school concerns.
- Etc.

Environment: *(Those things at the location of the tournament.)*

- New city or state.
- Uncomfortable tournament site.
- Attitudes of the sponsor and/or participants.
- Rude spectators.
- Forgot equipment.
- Waiting to fight.
- Waiting between fights.
- Don't understand the rules.
- Etc.

Post-Fight: *(Anything that carries over from one tournament to the next.)*

- Bad overall experience.
- Anger at coaches, judges, competitors, etc.
- Disappointment with performance.
- Depression and loss of self-confidence from losing.

- Anxiety about maintaining a winning status after winning the last tournament.
- Injury.
- Etc.

Think ahead and don't let these types of things affect your performance. Learn to expect anything and everything, stay calm, and use good organization and planning. Let your personal goals guide you. Don't be a superficial fighter concerned and worried about anything and everything. Realize that in competition, there are many factors besides you and an opponent that can affect your performance; judges, coaches, spectators, media people, etc.

> **How your thoughts and feelings translate into action determines your effectiveness.**

7. How did you prepare yourself mentally while training? Did it help you during competition? Why or why not?

   I didn't do any special "mental" exercises while training. I need to start doing them because I became frustrated while fighting.

Many martial artists don't pay enough attention to their mental outlook and attitude toward competition. Learning to be a focused and confident fighter is not always easy. Include in your training exercises that will enhance your mental powers. Use this question to monitor your progress.

8. How did you prepare yourself mentally the day of the fight? Did it help you during competition? Why or why not?

   I found a quiet spot with no one else around and spent about 20 minutes doing meditation and visualization exercises. This helped me to stay calm and to focus.

On the day of competition, don't just warm up your body, prepare your mind as well. The focus needed to compete at your best starts way before you actually fight. Monitor how your mental outlook before competition affects your overall performance.

9. Make a list of the areas you need to improve on?

   1. Use the time between when I arrive at the tournament until I fight to focus on my goals and strategy.
   2. Do not get nervous and apprehensive!

Once you have answered all of the first eight questions, make a general list of the areas that you need to improve on. Use this list as a guide to plan your future workouts.

Conclusion

You don't want to rely on just skill alone to make you a successful fighter. You must have the mental fortitude to use good planning. Good planning includes studying how the mind works while fighting. Earlier chapters of the A.Y.F.M. dealt with your performance at the physical level, giving you information about which techniques, tactics, and attributes you're capable of using or cannot use very effectively. Improvement in your execution of fighting techniques and the improvement of your win record cannot occur without improving your mental approach to fighting.

By doing a mental evaluation of how your mind works as you fight, you can determine the negative or positive effects of your thoughts and emotions. Once you know how your mind works, you can then plan your workouts and sparring sessions so that you can become a confident, disciplined and highly skilled fighter. Being "cool, calm, and collected" when it comes to fighting is the only way to be!

Mixed Martial Arts Fighter and Coach, Neal Rowe, of Sacan Martial Arts

Chapter Nine

"The way you train is the way you react."

Benny "The Jet" Uroquidez

How To Improve Your Training

The design of each level of evaluation is to help find specific areas of your fighting that need improvement. After identifying these areas, then it's time to set your training goals. This chapter shows you how to turn your training goals into training routines with specific objectives. Once you have specific training objectives than meeting your "fighting" goals will happen! When it comes to planning your workouts, the A.Y.F.M. gives you a tremendous advantage. For as much as the A.Y.F.M. tells you what you do, how often you do it, and how effective you are, it also tells you what you need to work on in your training.

Without "great" workouts you can't become a "great" fighter -- never take workout planning for granted! By having "structured" workouts your training time becomes much more productive and you'll achieve your goals in a shorter amount of time.

This chapter shows you how to use the A.Y.F.M. *Workout Plan* to organize your training goals and objectives into an effective personal training regimen.

Before learning how to use the *Workout Plan* you must understand the following:

1. How workouts (or classes) are generally structured.
2. The six main categories that make up "fighting."
3. The six main ways to improve your training.
4. The six main types of training.

The Class Structure

Most martial arts classes are generally structured around these four main activities (though not particularly in this order);

1. Warm Up
2. Review Old Material
3. New Material
4. Some Type Of Sparring

The instructor usually has some kind of objective or purpose in mind for each class. The objectives of the class may go something like this:

1. Warm Up	Stretching, line drills with kicking and punching.
2. Review Old Material	Re-practice backfist and backfist counters.
3. New Material	Learn spinning back kick, target areas for spinning back kick, and defenses for spinning back kick.

There are two main objectives to this class, to reinforce knowledge and skill of the "backfist" and to give new knowledge and skill in the form of a back kick. Every class or workout that you plan should have clear "objectives" as to what you want to achieve for that workout.

Even if you call up a martial arts friend and say, "Let's get together and work on our kicks," you've set an objective for that workout and that is to work on your kicking skills.

The workout with your friend would be much more effective if you would first have an overall goal that you're trying to achieve; with a date or a number of workouts for achieving that goal; and define a way for testing or knowing that you have achieved your goal. Here's how the workout with your friend would look with some planning:

Main Goal: To improve my ability to land kicks by 30%.
Time To Achieve Goal: Two months.
How To Test The Results Of These Workouts: Videotape and analysis three sparring sessions.
Workout Objective: Improve kicking speed.
Specific Exercises: (List specific exercises or drills and how much time per-exercise.)

The main goal in the above example is very specific. By having already done several A.Y.F.M. analyses you would know how many more kicks you would have to score with in order to achieve a 30% increase. The time set to achieve this 30% increase is two months. It's very important not only to set realistic goals but also to set realistic dates for achieving those goals. Once you established your main training goal and the time frame to achieve that goal, than plan each individual workout with the specific objective(s) for that workout and the specific exercises that you should do for that workout.

Understanding workout structure and planning is essential to using the *Workout Plan*.

Six Main Categories Of Fighting

Everything related to fighting or sparring falls under these *Six Main Categories Of Fighting*. It's from these six categories that you'll learn to base your workouts. By going through the analysis process you'll find specific skills that you need to work on in each of the six categories. To meet your full potential as a fighter, be sure to do adequate training in each of the six areas. Here are the six main categories from which to plan your workouts:

Training Category	Description
1. **Technique Usage**	How to use a technique and when to use it.
2. **Movement**	How to position the body in order to land techniques or to avoid being hit.
3. **Reaction To Opponent**	How to counter, meet, or avoid the opponent's attack.
4. **Attributes**	Conditioning - speed, power, timing, precision, reaction time, nutrition, etc.
5. **Strategies & Tactics**	Gathering information to generate and use tactics and strategies.
6. **Emotions**	Discipline, concentration, focus, fear, anxiety, attitude, etc.

Six General Ways To Improve Training

As you consider ways in which to upgrade your training, study the following six general methods to improve your training:

1. Increase time training, sparring, and competing.
2. Increase the intensity of training (increased repetitions and/or different types of drills).
3. Improve research and planning.

4. Use better equipment.
5. Seek out better and/or different training opportunities, coaches, and training partners.
6. Continue to analyze your fighting.

Don't get it in your mind that the only ways to improve are to "do more" and to do it "more often" (which doesn't always lead to doing it better). You can overtrain. Find a good balance between working out and doing research and planning (including analyzing your own fights and other martial artists' fights). There are hundreds of ways you can supplement your martial arts training with such things as reading books on martial arts, weight lifting, studying nutrition, etc.

After you have determined your training goals and objectives, use the six general ways to improve your training to help guide your progress. Fox example, if you decide that you have a problem with defending techniques directed to the left side of your body, than you can use some or all of the six general areas of training in this way:

1. Increase time training - allocate a larger portion of training (assign a time period like two months) to doing different defensive drills to the left side.
2. Add more and different defensive drills.
3. Improve research - find out how other styles defend that area.
4. Use protective equipment that allows training partners to make contact to that area.
5. Seek out the help of an instructor with excellent defensive skills for suggestions.
6. Analyze your defensive skills on videotape to find specific things you're doing wrong.

Six Types Of Training

Before you begin to use the *Workout Plan* you should also be aware of the six different types of training. All martial arts training fall under these six categories. As you plan workouts make use of all six types of training:

1. **Partner Cooperation** - you and your training partner practice a specific technique and/or drill with no interference in the execution; used primarily to first learn a technique, drill, combination, etc.

2. **Partner Interruption** - you and your partner agree to work on a specific technique, drill, combination, etc. but one partner makes it more difficult for the technique or application of a drill to be completed by disturbing the rhythm or execution of the technique/drill.

3. **Limited Sparring** - you and your partner set up certain conditions for your sparring, you may decide to just use hands, or one person use hands and the other use feet, etc.

4. **Free Sparring** - very few limitations put on the exchange of techniques, except those rules needed to ensure safety.

5. **Solo** - training by yourself with or without equipment.

6. **Lecture or classroom** - gathering knowledge by listening, reading, taking notes, or watching videos, etc.

Any one of these or all of these can include training equipment.

The Workout Plan

The workout plan is your program for success! This is where you'll express your goals and how to achieve them. The A.Y.F.M. assumes that your ultimate goal is to fulfill your potential as a martial artist. How you achieve that potential and how you exactly define your potential is up to you. Perhaps, you want to be a full-contact champion or want to be the best fighter in your school or style. Whatever your goals are, you'll achieve them much faster and with better understanding if you use the *Workout Plan*.

Each level of evaluation identifies areas of your fighting that needs improvement. The *Workout Plan* is designed to extrapolate from the evaluation worksheets those aspects of fighting that you need to work on. Those areas of fighting that you identify as needing work become your secondary goals. The secondary goals are areas of fighting that you need to work on in order to meet your primary goals (and to fulfill your potential as a fighter). Before you start to use the *Workout Plan* you need to be clear about your goals.

Primary and Secondary Goals

As stated earlier, the A.Y.F.M. assumes that your primary goal or your "ultimate" goal is to fulfill your potential as a martial artist! Many martial artists practice for physical fitness or for self-defense, but if you're willing to put yourself through the rigors of the A.Y.F.M., than you're surely interested in much more than "exercise." Perhaps, you never really gave much thought to an "ultimate" goal or to why you practice martial arts, but the A.Y.F.M. is most useful when you have an ultimate goal.

The ultimate goal decides the course of your training, and no workout plan is useful without knowing what you're trying to achieve. The *Workout Plan* asks you to describe your "ultimate" goal. Besides the ultimate goal, the A.Y.F.M. recognizes a set of "secondary goals" that are common to all fighters' pursuit of excellence. These secondary goals include:

Secondary Goals

- Increase win record.
- Increase technique usage (be able to score with a greater variety of techniques).
- Increase scoring percentage (be able to score more often).
- Increase skill (attributes).
- Increase tactical and strategic abilities.
- Become a superior fighter (explained in chapter thirteen).
- Etc.

The *Workout Plan* doesn't list secondary goals. Instead, secondary goals are translated into specific objectives. The objectives are what you plan your workouts around.

The Workout Plan:

1. Make clear your goals and objectives.
2. Break your goals down into specific exercises.
3. Test the results of your workouts.

Completing The Workout Plan

Workout Plan

Name: _David Staley_   Date: _1/10/98_ Workout #: _1_

Ultimate Goal: _To meet my full potential as a fighter!_

Main objective(s): At the completion of _8_ training sessions I will have learned, or be able to do, know, etc. the following;

1. _Learn to better control the pace of the fight._
2. _Learn to quickly interpret how each opponent uses "pace" against me._
3. _Realize an association between an improvement in my ability to control the pace of a fight, with an increase in scoring %._

Objective(s) for this workout:

1. _To practice drills and exercises that isolate_
2. _certain aspects of pace including footwork_
3. _and intensity of attacking and defending_

	Time:	Exercises & Drills:
1.	20	Warm up and stretching
2.	20	Punching bag drills - work above my normal pace
3.	20	Footwork drills - in and out, side to side, ect. vary
X.		my pace, rhythm, cadence, etc.
4. X.	20	Sparring drills: 1. having training partner rush in w/ attacks
6.		2. I will rush my training partner w/ attacks
7.		3. Have training partner vary his pace and
8.		I will concentrate on staying above it.
5. 6.	45	Evaluate other fighters use of pace on video
10.		tape using A.Y.F.M.

Evaluation: _During sparring use pace to my advantage to control the fight. Video tape myself sparring_

Materials Needed:
Stop watch, punching bag, double-end bag
Video taped fights of other fighters

Reference Material:
Analyze Your Fighting Method

The *Workout Plan* is very similar to the lesson plans that school teachers use. Teachers divide the subject curriculum for the whole course of study into separate lesson plans. Instead of a curriculum to work from, you have two different types of guides to plan workouts. The first is your goals, and the second is the results of your breakdown analyses. Review the results from your analyses and evaluations and take from them specific aspects of fighting to work on that are consistent with your goals.

These specific aspects of fighting become your training objectives. The training objectives are listed at the top of your *Workout Plan*. For example, if after analyzing your kicks you find that you often lose your balance while kicking and have a poor recovery of your kicking leg, your training objective could be; *"To learn to maintain good balance before, during, and after kicking, and to improve the recovery of my kicking leg."* Your next objective could then be to improve the scoring percentage of your kicks from twenty five percent to forty five percent.

Use one *Workout Plan* sheet for each workout. Take your time and complete each part of the plan. The following will explain in detail how to complete the *Workout Plan*.

1. Complete the general information at the top. Including your ultimate goal (what you want to achieve as a martial artist), your main objectives for this set of workouts, and how many workouts that are needed to achieve your objectives.

Name: *Frank Jones*   Date *12/9/97* Workout #: *6*

Ultimate Goal: *To meet my full potential as a martial artist*

Main objective(s): At the completion of *18* training sessions I will have learned, or be able to do, know, etc.;

1. *To increase the effectiveness of my defense*
2. *To decrease the number of times I defend myself*
3. *from an average of 54 times per fight to below 40.*

2. Clearly explain what skill or skills you'll be working on for this particular workout. This becomes your workout objective(s).

Objective(s) for this workout:

1. *To improve blocking skills without movement*
2. *To improve blocking skills with movement*
3. _____

3. The third section is for listing what drills and exercises you'll do to achieve your workout objectives. Describe the specific exercises and how much time for each drill.

	Time:	Exercises & Drills:
1.	*20*	*Warm up and stretching*
2.	*15*	*Practice blocking movements holding weights*
3.	*30*	*Stand against the wall and have training partner*
4.		*throw punches at me to practice blocking without movement*
5.	*30*	*Have training partner throw techniques at me*
6.		*while I block not throwing any counter punches*

4. Use the "evaluation" section to describe how you'll know that you've achieved your workout objective. This section is very important! You must have a way of knowing that you've achieved your objectives!

Evaluation: *Videotape six two minute rounds of sparring, the analyze my blocking abilities.*

5. The last two sections are for listing specific materials or supplies that you need for this workout and to note any reference materials (books, magazines, videos, etc.) that you want to study.

Materials Needed:

Reference Material:

Conclusion:

How you perform in competition is directly related to how you train. How you train is dependent upon how much planning you put into your workouts. Therefore, effective workout planning leads to an effective fighter. The A.Y.F.M. *Workout Plan* forces you to be clear about your goals and how you'll achieve them.

Chapter Ten

How To Become A Strategist

"Knowing that opponents are constantly trying to note one's habits and weaknesses, it is obvious that a conscious effort must be made to give variety to one's game."

Bruce Lee

When you anticipate fighting in a tournament or sparring a classmate, what goes through your mind in terms of how you'll fight? Could it be something like this; "I'm going to be aggressive, no one can stop my roundhouse kick! Mark Jones isn't going to beat me this time, his luck has run out! When he hit me with that back kick in the last tournament to beat me, it was a fluke; he can't beat me again. I've been training hard, I'm in shape and ready to go!" Does this kind of psychobabble sound familiar -- "I'm going to win because I'm going to win" kind of talk. What kind of world would we be living in today if Dwight D. Eisenhower tried to win World War II with this kind of shallow planning?

War involves planning. Planning based on knowing as much as possible about your enemy and about your own skills and resources as possible. Strategy isn't just saying, "Let me try this or let me try that." Strategy is a plan of action based on factual information. Anything less is almost like fighting in the dark. Maybe you'll hit something and maybe you won't. Armies use spies and various other kinds of reconnaissance techniques to gather information to form strategic battle plans. You should do your own investigation of fighters before you compete against them.

This chapter shows you the following: (1) the difference between tactics and strategies, (2) how tactics and strategies work together, and (3) a structured methodology for turning tactics into well-planned strategies. To help form strategies, the A.Y.F.M. gives you a comprehensive "*Tactics Catalogue.*" You'll use the *Tactics Catalogue* (explained in chapter twelve) and the *Strategy Worksheet* to construct "battle plans" based on the following four categories of fighters:

> 1. **Against the two general types of fighters (the defensive fighter and the offensive fighter).**
> 2. **Against fighters of different martial arts styles.**
> 3. **Against certain body types and attributes (tall, short, fast, powerful, etc.)**
> 4. **Against a specific fighter (that you have particular knowledge about).**

How much knowledge you have about your opponent determines which category of fighter you use. If you only know the opponent's style than you'll formulate a strategy based on that styles common strengths and weaknesses. If you're able to videotape your opponents competing than you can make a detailed study of his performance by using the A.Y.F.M.

Before you can start formulating strategies, you must understand how strategy and tactics work together.

How Strategy and Tactics Work Together

When a beginning martial artist spars he is essentially experimenting. He'll throw techniques and see what happens. The intermediate martial artist can use techniques and tactics that he has confidence in, and will show signs of developing a personal "style" based on past success. The advanced martial artist is fully aware of the use of tactics and how and when to use them. The superior martial artist can go a step further and formulate and execute "strategies." That is, the ability to take in as much information as possible about his competitor, and knowing his own strengths and weaknesses, can plan the most effective way to defeat the opponent. His plan or "strategy" for beating the opponent is essentially a list of specific tactics. This forms the basis for the difference between "strategy" and "tactics." **Tactics are what you use to execute a strategy. A strategy is an overall battle plan.**

Most fighters are a mixture of tactician and strategist. They train, enter a tournament, and use their strengths in whatever tactical ways their training has engraved into their nervous system. For example, a fighter may like to use foot fakes to set up his backfist, and he does this in every fight he has, even if his opponent is very good at recognizing fakes and stopping backfists. So this fighter's whole strategy is to use his fakes to land backfists. His strategy can be illustrated in this way:

Strategy: Win by using foot fakes and backfists.

Tactical Breakdown:

a. foot fakes
b. quick backfists

Hopefully, the fighter in the above example would use more techniques and tactics as he fought, but this example makes the point that most fighters don't use well-planned strategies, and are limited in their use of tactics.

A better, but not complete strategy, would go something like this; "I'm going to look the guy in the eyes to intimidate him, and use very aggressive gestures and movement to keep him from feeling comfortable. Then I'll throw a lot of hand and body fakes to score with my fast front, side, and roundhouse kicks."

Here's how this strategy can be broken down:

Strategy: Win by showing intimidation and aggression along with hand and body fakes to score with kicks.

Tactical Breakdown:

a. intimidating looks
b. aggressive gestures
c. movement meant to pressure the opponent
d. hand and body fakes
e. fast kicks

The above strategy is more complete than the first example because it uses "mental" tactics such as "intimidation" along with more "distraction" tactics (faking). But it's still limited because it concentrates on only one type of techniques (kicks) and doesn't take into account other factors such as type of fighter, the opponent's style, or special attributes that the opponent has, etc.

Remember, strategy is a "fight" plan that contains a set of tactics. The use of strategy will greatly enhance your fighting ability, because in order to formulate strategies, you must also have a strong knowledge of fighting tactics. Tactics define how you use techniques. The ability to use a number of tactics greatly increases your chances to defeat any type of fighter in front of you regardless of the opponent's style, body shape, or skill level. Ideally, it's your "thinking" that will defeat opponents -- your ability to choose tactics quickly and use them successfully.

Strategy, as something you plan before you fight, trains your mind to put yourself into certain situations with different types of opponents, which in turn also directs your training to carrying out your mission (meaning your strategy). **You'll be a much better fighter if you change your training from being "technique" or "tactic" oriented to being "strategy" oriented!**

Formulating Strategies

The basic methodology behind forming strategies is this; **exploit your strengths, guard against your weaknesses, while avoiding your opponent's strengths, and exploiting his weaknesses.** The purpose of strategy is to give yourself an edge over your opponents by gathering information (before the fight) and using that information to increase your chances of winning.

Since strategies are a compilation of information, you must have some minimal knowledge about the person you're going to fight. If you're a karate point fighter or a Tae Kwon Do tournament fighter than you know you're likely to fight karate or Tae Kwon Do stylists. So in your strategy planning you can make certain assumptions about the "style" of fighters you're competing against.

You can also assume that you'll face at least two "types" of fighters, that being either an "offensive" or a "defensive" fighter. Offensive fighters are aggressive and attack more than they defend. Defense fighters defend more than they attack.

The optimal strategy-planning situation is to have detailed information about the fighters that you'll be facing, by having them on videotape.

The A.Y.F.M. will show you how to form strategies based on the amount of knowledge you have. Before you start to use the *Strategy Worksheet* and the *Tactical Catalogue* the following four sections will give you more information about forming strategies based on: martial arts style, type of fighter, body size, attributes, and specific fighters (that you have a lot of information about).

Style Specific Strategies

If you know what style your opponent is practicing you can make some assumptions about how he'll fight. It's important to remember though, that there can be a vast amount of individual preference even within a style. Still, every fighter is an expression of the style he studies.

It's beyond the scope of the A.Y.F.M. to explain why different styles of martial arts do what they do, but it is important to know three aspects of "style" that are pertinent to forming fighting strategies. These three aspects of martial art "style" or "system" include technique preference, range, and tactical preference.

Technique Preference: Some styles prefer to use circular techniques while others prefer straight-line techniques. Still other styles prefer kicking techniques over hand techniques, etc. Use tactics that inhibit or counter the technique preferences of your opponent's style. For example, if a style prefers to kick than be prepared to use tactics against kicks, such as jamming or grabbing the kicking leg.

Tactical Preference: Just as each style has certain techniques that it prefers to employ, there are preferential ways to use those techniques. For example, if a style has an emphasis on elbow techniques than it will employ certain tactics designed to help the elbow hit, such as grabbing and pulling the opponent into elbow range. Another style may prefer to use low line techniques (below the waist) and tactics with the purpose of robbing the opponent of movement and the ability to kick. Use tactics that avoid and/or counter the tactical preferences of your opponent's style. If you're up against a style that prefers to draw you into a mid-section reverse punch, use tactics that counter this. Such tactics could involve not allowing your opponent to drawn you in while using quick side-to-side movements and beating the reverse punch with quicker front arm or front leg techniques such as the backfist or front kick.

Fighting Range: Most types of martial arts tournaments emphasize one or two ranges of fighting. Karate tournaments emphasize the kicking and hand ranges, whereas judo tournaments emphasize the throwing and grappling ranges. Mixed Martial Arts and Thai Boxing are examples of the few types of competition with emphasis more than two ranges of fighting including; kicking, punching, elbow/knee ranges, and grappling/groundwork.

Techniques always have an optimal range. The fighter that can control the range and pace of the fight essentially controls the fight. Learn to fight from a number of different ranges and force the opponent into his most uncomfortable range.

Attributes & Body Size

As explained in chapter seven, attributes as pertaining to the martial arts include but are not limited to the following:

1. Speed
2. Power
3. Timing
4. Mobility
5. Precision
6. Body type (tall, short, strong, etc.)

Be prepared to use strategies against the advantages that your opponent has based on his attributes. This should be a very important part of your training -- what to do against a very fast opponent, or how to fight a tall opponent who has a long reach, etc. Pay particular attention to how the opponent uses his "attributes" not just that he's powerful or tall. In other words, is he a tall defensive fighter who waits for an attack and then uses his reach to score, or maybe he's extremely fast and aggressive and loves to keep his opponent's confused, etc.?

Every fighter has advantages and disadvantages by virtue of his attributes. As you guard against his strengths, use your strong attributes to take advantage of his weak attributes. If you have strong kicks and he doesn't have very good movement, than use your kicks to keep him off balance.

Use the *Strategy Worksheet* and the *Tactical Catalogue* to find what will counter advantages or disadvantages created by attributes.

Types Of Fighters

There are two general types of fighters including, "offensive" fighters and "defensive" fighters.

Offensive fighters are aggressive and attack more often than they defend. They take the fight to the opponent, forcing the opponent to act defensively and to counter punch before he's ready. Defensive fighters like to wait, taking their time to draw the opponent into counter techniques, and are generally good at exploiting the opponent's weaknesses.

Despite the fact that there are "offensive" and "defensive" types, there really is no clear way to categorize "types" of fighters in the martial arts. The A.Y.F.M. doesn't attempt to develop "categories" of fighters either. To develop categories of fighters you would have to assign martial artists to certain groups according to physical make-up (attributes), and tactical preferences (style). It's easy to see how this could become confusing very quickly -- some fighters are known as "kickers," others for being "fast," and still others for being "very tough and powerful," etc. What's more important than "categorizing" fighters is recognizing tendencies in tactics. That is, it's important to identify a fighter's dominant tactical base in order to formulate a strategy against it. Perhaps a fighter loves to use fakes including shifting footwork in order to confuse his opponent. It's not as important to place this fighter into a category such as "shifty," as it is to quickly recognize that this is how he fights, and that his "shiftiness" is designed to make you feel uncomfortable and vulnerable to attack.

The whole concept of "type" of fighter then, is "strategy" based. "Type of fighter," means that the fighter is more likely to use certain tactics based on that person's strengths and personal preferences. Remember, it's not enough to know that a person is "fast" you need to know how he uses speed. Is he a fast defensive fighter using quick counter punches, or is he an offensive speedster blitzing his opponents with lightening punches and combinations? It's not sufficient to have tactics in your repertoire to deal with speed, you must understand how "speed" is used. This is advanced thinking and planning in fighting! Also, remember that, **every tactic has a counter tactic. The secret to winning is executing the "right" tactic at a superior moment.**

To increase your chances of using the "right" tactic is why you need to plan strategies. If you want to create strategies based on "types" of fighters, know the strengths and weaknesses of your classification and how to take advantage of them. Keep in mind as you place fighters into categories that you should always consider individual differences.

Dominate Strategy Defines "Type" Of Fighter.

Specific Fighter

Forming a strategy against a specific fighter means that you know who you're going to fight and have accurate information about him. Obviously, the best information about a particular fighter would come from a videotape of him fighting. This allows you to analyze how he fights in a complete manner and to clearly see what his favorite techniques are, what tactics he uses, along with any other information you choose to extract from the video. In this case, you would use the worksheets from the various levels of evaluation, the *Tactical Catalogue,* and the *Strategy Worksheet* to formulate and practice a strategy that you would use to defeat this particular fighter. If you don't have the fighter on videotape, use what information you know about him to form a strategy. Maybe you know his style, have seen him fight, or you may have fought him in the past, etc.

The Strategy Worksheet

Strategy Worksheet

Your Name: _Tim Dukeman_ Opponent's Name: _David Staley_
Style: _Shotokan_ Style: _Shorin-Ryu_

Type Of Fighter	You	Opponent	Range Preferences	You	Opponent
Offensive	✓		Hand		✓
Defensive		✓	Kicking	✓	
Other			Elbow/Knee		✓
Other			Grappling		

Your Tactical Preferences:

1. Use kicks to set-up hands
2. Spinning back fist followed by kicks
3. Pressure the opponent - throw alot of techniques

Opponent's Tactical Preferences:

1. Loves to throw hand combinations
2. Good counter puncher
3. Waits for attacks very cautious

Your Movement Patterns:

Move in and out - changing stances
Attacks more than defends

Opponent's Movement Patterns:

Stands ground and counter punches
Hardly moves back - good explosion forward

Your Attributes	Strengths	Weaknesses
Speed	✓	
Power		✓
Timing	✓	
Flexibility	✓	
Conditioning	✓	
Body Type	Tall	Thin
Other		

Opponent's Attributes	Strengths	Weaknesses
Speed	✓	
Power	✓	
Timing	✓	
Flexibility		✓
Conditioning		✓
Body Type	Tall	Muscular
Other		

Your Mental Disposition:

Move around nervous - but confident

Opponent's Mental Disposition:

Doesn't show any emotion, very focused

Additional Information About Opponent:

Heard from the grapevine that his right ankle has been giving him trouble.

Formulate Your Strategy Below:

Use good in and out movement to avoid his hand combinations (control distance)
Control the pace of the fight, jam him, circle him, etc. to avoid counter punch.
Practically run him over if that's what it takes to break his
concentration
Talk to him before, during, and between rounds if possible just
enough to break his focus.

Strategies are pre-fight plans detailing how to defeat your opponents. Strategies are based on all the information that you're able to gather about how your opponents are likely to fight. Creating strategies involves two main steps:

1. Gathering information about the strengths and weaknesses of both you and your opponents.

2. Choosing tactics that take advantage of your opponent's physical and emotional strengths and weaknesses, while exploiting your strengths and guarding against your weaknesses.

The *Strategy Worksheet* helps you formulate complete strategies. A complete strategy considers the strengths and weaknesses of you and your opponent on both a physical and emotional level.

Completing The Strategy Worksheet

The *Strategy Worksheet* asks you to do three things; first log information about yourself, secondly log information about your opponent, and finally to create your strategy. Follow these steps to complete the worksheet:

1. Complete the first section of the worksheet with your name and style, and your opponent's name and style.

Your Name:		Opponent's Name:	
Style:		Style:	

2. Complete the second section of the worksheet by placing an "X" in the appropriate blank to indicate what type of fighter you are, what type of fighter your opponent is, your range preference, and the opponent's range preference.

Type Of Fighter	You	Opponent	Range Preferences	You	Opponent
Offensive			Hand	X	
Defensive	X	X	Kicking		X
Other			Elbow/Knee		
Other			Grappling		

3. To complete the third section of the worksheet, list the technique and tactical preferences for yourself and the opponent. *(Remember it's not enough to know what techniques the opponent likes to use, you also must know how he uses them tactically.)*

Your Tactical Preferences:

1. *Use stop kicks to set-up hands*
2. *Covering up and then exploding with punch*
3. *Spinning backfist with hand and foot fakes*

Opponent's Tactical Preferences:

1. *Leans back often to throw*
2. *backfists and kicks*
3. *Loves to throw kicking combinations*

4. Complete the fourth section of the worksheet by detailing the movement patterns that you and your opponent use.

Your movement patterns:

Don't move very much at all

Counter puncher and stop kicks

Opponent's Movement Patterns:

Moves in circles throwing kicks

Uses a lot of spinning techniques

5. Complete the fifth section of the worksheet by placing an "X" in the appropriate blank indicating the strong and weak areas of your and the opponent's attributes, body type, and mental disposition while fighting.

Your Attributes	Strengths	Weaknesses	Opponent's Attributes	Strengths	Weaknesses
Speed			Speed	X	
Power		X	Power		
Timing	X		Timing		X
Flexibility	X		Flexibility	X	
Conditioning	S		Conditioning	X	
Body Type	Tall		Body Type	Tall	
Other			Other		

Your Mental Disposition:

Calm - love to compete

Opponent's Mental Disposition:

Nervous always moving around

6. The next section of the worksheet is for listing any other information about your opponent that could help you form a more complete strategy.

Additional Information About Opponent:

He scores 60% of the time with kicks

7. The last section of the worksheet is for creating the strategy that you'll use to defeat the opponent. *(Feel free to create as many strategies as you like, then choose the one that you'll memorize and practice in your training.)* The strategy should use your strengths to exploit the opponent's weaknesses, while at the same time guard against the opponent's strengths and your weaknesses. Use the *Tactics Catalogue* from chapter twelve to help you find tactics to use in your strategy.

Formulate Your Strategy Below:

1. Isolate his movement by cutting him off
2. Keep him from kicking by controlling the distance - move in on him constantly.
3. When he moves back to throw a backfist or a kick - draw him in to counter punches and other techniques.

Some Key Points To Keep In Mind

♦ As you follow the steps involved in completing the *Strategy Worksheet* don't forget to consider the mental aspects of fighting. Whereas strategies are made up of tactics and tactics are made up of techniques, nothing will work without proper mental preparation, focus, and attitude. **Then you have to employ the strategies you create.** Chapter nine, on doing a mental or retrospective analysis of fighting, discussed the fact that most actions in fighting are the result of an emotional response -- such as anger. When you have control of your emotional responses you can use strategy. Without control of your thoughts, feelings, and emotions, you'll respond emotionally not logically. Fighting at its highest level is the logical use of knowledge backed up by uninhibited reaction to change tactics as necessary. Continue working on your mental powers to be disciplined in emotion, tactical choice, and strategy formation and use.

♦ There's an old axiom that states, "No plan survives the battle field." This means that no matter how well you plan something, nothing ever goes 100% as you planned. Fighting is dynamic, constantly changing, and using strategy helps you plan for the unexpected. It takes the mystery out of facing new opponents and calms the fear of the unexpected while at the same time making your martial arts experience more rewarding because you'll come to an advanced understanding of the dynamics of fighting.

♦ Don't make a strategy the night before a competition and expect to be able to stick to it the next day. Create the strategy weeks ahead of time and plan your training around the strategy, that way when it's time to compete the strategy is already a part of you.

♦ Use the *Tactics Catalogue* (chapter twelve) to help you develop new tactical approaches to fighting. Practice new tactics during your training and don't be afraid to use them in sparring and competition. Every time you compete you not only want to "win" but you should also be interested in learning more about fighting.

♦ Not every opponent will react to your tactics in the same way. Expect the unexpected and be ready for change.

♦ As you analyze and re-analyze how your strategies are working, remember to note why your tactics didn't work. Pay particular attention to the signals you're sending opponents such as body language and telegraphing. You should only be sending "intentional" messages to your opponent. Always convey a sense of control.

♦ As you analyze videotaped fights of your opponents pay attention to how other fighters reacted to your opponents while fighting. See what tactics they're able to score with and those that failed. You may decide to use some of the same tactics.

♦ Don't overload your strategies with tactics, you'll just end up forgetting what you planned to do. Keep the strategies simple and train them to the point that you won't abandon them under the pressure of competition. Remember to include in your strategies tactics that affect the opponent mentally.

Case Study

Here's an additional example of how to form a strategy. Fighter (1), Mark, is planning a strategy against fighter (2), Frank.

Fighter #1: Mark

Style:	Mo Do Kwon
Strengths:	Very fast front leg roundhouse kicks (roundhouse kicks have a 38% chance of landing), good back kick. Mark scores 70% of the time with kicks and 30% of the time with hands.
Attributes:	Tall and has deceptively long kicks.
Tactical Preferences:	Likes to wait, doesn't initiate the action, only attacks 31% of the time.
Type Of Fighter:	Defensive.
Weaknesses:	Doesn't score well with hands, doesn't like being in the hand range. Has trouble setting up his kicks against aggressive fighters. Doesn't try to control the pace of the fight.
Mentally	Becomes worried when he gets behind in points.

Fighter #2: Frank

Style:	Modern Karate
Strengths:	Scores 73% of the time with hand techniques, 50% of which are reverse punches. Is good at controlling the distance.
Attributes:	Strong build, very powerful. Has quick footwork for someone who is stocky.
Tactical Preferences:	Likes to throw kicks and then charge in with powerful reverse punches. Throws occasional backfists (20% of the time).
Type Of Fighter:	Offensive
Weaknesses:	Doesn't have a strong defense. Doesn't vary his tactics from those described above.
Mentally	Uses intimidating looks, has the sleeves cut off his uniform to show his big arms, carries a big ego.

Strategy Formation:

To form a strategy against Frank, Mark should first get an overall picture of who he's fighting. Frank isn't hard to figure out. He's aggressive in both action and ego and usually uses the same tactics. So with the *Tactical Catalogue* in hand, Mark needs to first see how he can use his strengths against Frank. Mark knows that he has fast kicks, so he needs to score first before Frank becomes too aggressive. Frank doesn't use fakes and he doesn't seem bothered by them either, so Mark also decides that when Frank does become aggressive he'll jam him and angle away from Frank's strong reverse punch. This should draw Frank into another kick. If Mark can't jam Frank, which could happen since Frank has such good footwork, Mark realizes that he may have to go toe to toe with Frank. Mark's advantage in this case is his longer reach. If he must go toe-to-toe, Mark feels that he has to throw more techniques than Frank, to increase his chances of scoring and to keep Frank contained (again because of Frank's good footwork).

To take advantage of Frank's weak defensive skills, Mark not only plans to throw more techniques than Frank but to also use a greater variety of techniques. Mark also realized while studying Frank that no one ever tries to grab him or to off balance him (probably because Frank is so intimidating). By trying to grab Frank, Mark may invoke an emotional response from Frank that may break his concentration (and perhaps his ego).

Mark feels that the above tactics in his strategy for fighting Frank are the correct ones because they use his strengths, his height and fast kicks, against Frank's strengths, which are his aggressive power and footwork. Mark also picked tactics that will help him face his own weaknesses such as fighting toe-to-toe. He also plans to use tactics that take advantage of Frank's weak defense. He'll even test Frank's ego to hopefully cause him to doubt himself. So with this information on his *Strategy Worksheet*, Mark is ready to set up his training routines so that he can specifically train to defeat Frank.

Here's one way to summarized Mark's strategy at the bottom of the *Strategy Worksheet*:

1. Use kicks to score first before Frank becomes too aggressive.
2. Jam Frank when he becomes aggressive and move away from the reverse punch.
3. When moving away from Frank's reverse punch draw him into a kick.
4. Use longer reach if forced to go toe-to-toe.
5. In the toe-to-toe situation throw more techniques than Frank.
6. Stay confident and focused, don't fall for Frank's intimidation, break his ego.

Exercises

Create a strategy that would defeat the following opponents. Use the *Strategy Worksheet* and the *Tactical Catalog*.

1. This fighter is about five feet nine inches in height and around one hundred ninety pounds. He's quick and loves to throw combinations -- 70% of his attacks involve a combination. He scores with almost 60% of the combinations that he throws (this is very good). His combinations are evenly divided between hand combinations and hand and foot combinations. He doesn't use kicks in combinations. His defense relies entirely on trying to counter punch, he rarely tries to block and counter. He seems to have trouble blocking mid-section kicks.

2. This fighter is a master of deception. He loves to use fakes, averaging almost 60 fakes a fight with 40% of them setting up a successful score. He also uses surprise techniques including flying kicks and spinning kicks (about one out of five techniques he throws). From time to time, he doesn't even use a fighting stance he'll just walk around the ring, or walk right at the opponent -- he can still attack by doing this. He loves to invoke an emotional response from his opponents. His defense relies on leaning back and going out of bounds. He's vulnerable to combinations, 70% of the techniques scored against him were from combinations.

Conclusion

Strategies are pre-fight plans based on information, the more detective work you do the more information you'll have, which translates into a more detailed strategy against your opponents. So, a complete strategy is based on an intense study of your opponent. This can only be done by having the opponent on videotape and subjecting him to the four levels of evaluation. If you have limited information about the opponent, than base your strategy on what you have, even if all you know is the opponent's style, attributes, type of fighter, or some combination of these.

Success comes from knowledge first, followed by preparation (training) and focused effort on goals!

The A.Y.F.M. *Tactical Catalogue* and *Strategy Worksheet* gives you the tools to form devastatingly effective strategies.

Chapter Eleven

"To me, ultimately, martial arts means honestly expressing yourself, Now, it is very difficult to do."

Bruce Lee

Mixed Martial Arts

So far in this book no specific type of fighting has been emphasized, as the A.Y.F.M. is ultimately designed for any type of fighting from boxing to Judo and everything else in-between. Since Mixed Martial Arts (MMA) is one of the three fastest growing sports in the world both in participation of athletes and in fan base (along with soccer and lacrosse), it's appropriate to add some discussion about MMA to this book – as there's also a good chance that if you are reading this, than you are a MMA fighter or coach or are considering becoming one.

MMA is a combination of stand-up fighting or striking and grappling often referred to as "ground game." Stand-up fighting includes techniques such as; punches, elbows, kicks, and knee strikes while grappling techniques includes; clinching, submissions, joint locks, takedowns, and throws. In stand-up fighting the main goal is to injure or knockout the opponent with strikes. In grappling the ways to defeat an opponent increases beyond just striking to include the use of submission joint locks and chock holds. For a MMA fighter to reach a high level of competition he must be skilled in both stand-up and ground fighting!

As the A.Y.F.M. has made clear, the most important thing to do when you analyze fights it to translate as much of the action that you can into numbers. You don't want to just watch the fights because you're opinion and interpretation of the fight is always going to be biased based on your own experience and training. Bias is just a part of our human nature. The brain is a relational computer; it connects what it sees to what it knows. Truer objectivity comes from collaboration of different backgrounds and experiences. Fights that are transcribed into number are less bias. This is also why most professional MMA fighters have more than one type of coach who specializes in certain areas of fighting (such as boxing, wrestling, Brazilian jiu-jitsu, Muay Thai, and kickboxing) and why MMA fighting is so compelling and comprehensive.

Since MMA fighting is so complex it's best to analyze fights with a team. The fighter and coaches should watch the fights and complete the worksheets together. This is not to say that the general comments that are made while watching fights are not important. One coach commented that he thought his fighter was reluctant to go "all out" in his ground and pound because he didn't want to become too tired to defend himself. If the fighter is there you can ask him if that is what he's really doing or not. How a fighter uses his energy is very important especially in MMA fights where rounds can last up to five minutes long.

Besides being highly skilled in both stand-up fighting and grappling mixed martial artists need to understand how to transition from stand-up to grappling while maintaining control of the opponent. This is where such tactics as clinching, use of the guard, passing the guard, and the ground and pound come into play.

It's also important for coaches to listen to how fighters explain what they did in a fight. When you here a fighter say, "I was trying to..." are they really telling the truth or are they making an excuse. Honesty makes champions! Especially being honest with yourself.

Like all of the worksheets in this book, this one serves as a guide to creating your own. Most coaches keep some kind of "fighter factsheet" or random notes; the challenge is to transform that into a more formal worksheet that all the fighter's coaches can use together.

The worksheet shown here is similar to the "**Fighter Comparison Worksheet**," in Chapter 7. This worksheet includes a section for comparing the strengths and weaknesses between fighters "transition game." Some of the other areas of MMA competition that should be compared include how fighters "control the cage" and "apply movement pressure (or forward pressure)." A good resource in which to see MMA statistics is the website www.fightmetric.com

Mixed Martial Arts Worksheet

Fighter #1: _____

Height: _____
Weight: _____
Reach: _____
Age: _____
Stance: _____
Fight Record: Win: _____ Loss: _____
　　　　　　　Draw: _____ Knockout: _____

Stand-Up

Strengths: _____

_____

_____

Weaknesses: _____

_____

_____

Ground Game

Strengths: _____

_____

_____

Weaknesses: _____

_____

_____

Transition Game

Strengths: _____

_____

_____

Weaknesses: _____

_____

_____

Fighter #2: _____

Height: _____
Weight: _____
Reach: _____
Age: _____
Stance: _____
Fight Record: Win: _____ Loss: _____
　　　　　　　Draw: _____ Knockout: _____

Stand-Up

Strengths: _____

_____

_____

Weaknesses: _____

_____

_____

Ground Game

Strengths: _____

_____

_____

Weaknesses: _____

_____

_____

Transition Game

Strengths: _____

_____

_____

Weaknesses: _____

_____

_____

Chapter Twelve

A.Y.F.M. Tactical Catalogue

      This catalogue of tactics and their definitions is an important supplement to your strategic planning. It's by no means a complete list of martial arts tactics and applies mostly to stand-up fighting. Add to the catalogue from your personal experiences any tactics that you know are missing. Don't just add tactics to the catalogue that you use. Even if you would never use the tactics you're adding, you want to be aware of them so that your opponent's can't use them against you.

      Use the *Tactical Catalogue* to help you complete the *Strategy Worksheet* from chapter eleven. The catalogue is made up of the following six tactical categories:

Tactic Categories	Description
1. **Attack Tactics**	Those tactics most likely used in an attack.
2. **Defensive Tactics**	Those tactics most likely used in defense.
3. **Distraction Tactics**	Tactics such as fakes, feints, draws, etc., used to distract the opponent from the "real" intent of a technique.
4. **Rules Tactics**	Tactics that use the rules of the competition in such a way as to help one win or gain an advantage.
5. **Attribute Tactics**	Tactics which change the use of speed, timing, footwork (mobility and direction), distance, power, and/or body size, etc.
6. **Nonspecific Tactics**	Those tactics that can be used in more than one situation.

Analyze Your Fighting Method
Tactical Catalogue

Attack Tactics

1. Straight Attack	Direct straight-line attack to the opponent.
2. Blitz	Charging at the opponent with many techniques.
3. Angular Attack	An attack that doesn't follow a straight line to the opponent.
4. The Walk	Move towards the opponent with normal walking steps - attacking when in range.
5. Hit Before (interception)	Attack before the opponent's attack (reading the opponent's intention, set point, and body language) "Beating him to the punch."
6. Hit During (counter punch)	Attack as the opponent attacks, taking a different angle that allows the avoidance of the opponent's attack but allows a hit to be made.
7. Hit After (follow the recovery)	After the opponent's technique has reached its maximum length immediately attack as the opponent recovers his arm or leg.
8. Hitting Limbs (uncommon targets)	Hitting arms, legs, and other targets that aren't usually thought of as such.
9. Drawing In	Creating an opportunity and target for the opponent to hit with the intent of causing the opponent to come into range to be attacked.
10. Drawing Away	Cause the opponent to "back-peddle" or lean back and then attack.
11. Progressive Combinations	Engage the opponent (in any manner) more than once -- with the real intention of attacking on the second or third engagement.
12. Immobilization (grabs)	Grab the opponent with the intention of creating a better chance of landing an attack.
13. Pushing	Force the opponent off balance temporarily to land an attack.
14. Alternations	Shifting between two different tactics in order to confuse the opponent as to which one you'll really attack with.
15. Raping	Fast slaps or short hits (usually done on the arms) designed to create a "freeze" in the opponent, to land an attack.
16. Foot Sneak	Move your foot toward the opponent without the opponent seeing it, to create less distance to attack, or move the foot back to create more distance.
17. Combinations	Attack with more than one technique.
18. Misdirection	Changing the direction of a technique as it goes towards the opponent.
19. Take A Hit	Let the opponent land a technique in order to land one or more counter hits.
20. Spinning	Turning the body around in a full circle and throwing a technique, as in a spinning backfist.

21. Reverse Direction	Techniques thrown in one direction and then are brought back the opposite direction and turned into another technique (hook punch is brought back and turned into a back fist).
22. The Hide	Throwing one technique and then hiding a fallow up technique behind the first. Example, *throw a backfist, keep the hand up into the opponent's eye area and then throw a reverse punch.*
23. The Lunge	Throw one technique as the opponent tries to move back, lunge far forward at the opponent with the same or another technique.
24. Pick Up & Slide	Used in kicking. Pick up the kicking leg, push off the supporting leg and finish kick.
25. Pendulum Kick	Kicking motion in which the front leg and back leg maintain the same distance from each other while kicking (until the back leg forms the base for the kick and the kick is extended to the target).
26. Pick Up and Drop	Kick without using much of a chamber to the kicking leg and let it drop to the floor.
27. Foot Shuffle	The back foot comes towards the front foot in a stance, usually after a fake, as the rear foot approaches the front - move the front foot forward in a quick motion recreating the stance and throwing a technique or combination.
28. Step Through	Throw a back arm or leg technique and let your back leg become your front leg. Techniques can be added at various times during the step through.
29. Step Through Lunge	As you step through with your back leg burst forward to cover a lot of distance and land a technique.
30. Slide Up-Lunge	Move the back leg up to the front leg and then burst forward into a stance covering a lot of distance and throwing a technique.
31. Multiple	Throw the same technique more than once (such as two or three jabs).
32. Throw And Drop	Throw one technique and drop your arms on the recovery to draw a response from the opponent and then counter hit.

Defensive Tactics

1. Counter Punch (or pass)	Moving slightly off the angle of an attack to counter attack (while not blocking the attack).
2. Covering Up	Using the arms and legs in such a way as to "cover" the body from attack.
3. Blocking	Stopping an attack with equal or greater force.
4. Parrying	Redirecting a punch or kicking attack off its line of direction.
5. Jamming	Moving in on an attack not allowing it to reach its maximum length. Used with covering up or blocking.
6. Moving	Moving your body in a direction to avoid the attack (backward, horizontal, to the side, diagonal)
7. Bobbing	Moving the head and shoulders up and down to cause the attack to miss.
8. Weaving	Moving the head and shoulders in a circular manner to cause the attack to miss.
9. Ducking	Moving directly under an attack to cause it to miss.
10. Slipping	Moving the head slightly so that the attack brushes over the shoulder.
11. Slapping	Slapping an attacking arm or leg as opposed to blocking or parrying it.
12. Pinning (trapping)	Trapping an arm or leg so that the opponent can't use it (usually against his own body).
13. Counter Hitting	Hitting the attacking arm or leg.
14. Clinching	One fighter wraps his arm or arms around the other fighter to keep the fighter from punching. Commonly seen in boxing
15. Reinforced Parry	One arm parries a technique while the other arm supports the parrying arm.
16. Recovery Parry	While recovering a technique you threw (such as a jab or cross) that arm changes into a parry (it doesn't fully recover, but changes into a parry).
17. Double Parry	Both arms parry the opponent's technique.
18. Catch	Stop the attack by "catching" it in the palm of your hand like a baseball glove would catch a baseball.
19. Fall Down	Fall to the floor so that the opponent can't score on you.

Distraction Tactics

Note: The distraction tactics listed here only include some of the most common.

1. Changing Stances	Switching to another stance or posture giving the appearance of using a new set of tactics.
2. Changing Postures	Starting with one posture and changing arm positions, head, leg, or body position, etc.
3. Weight Shifting	Changing weight from one leg to the other.
4. Various Body Motions	Any number of extraneous motions, such as waving the hands, holding one leg up, etc.
5. Fake Combinations	Using more than one type of fake preceding the real attack.
6. Fake High - Attack Low	Motion high with the head, body, hand, leg, or a combination of these with the real intent of hitting lower than the fake.
7. Fake Low - Attack High	Motion low with the head, body, hand, leg or a combination of these with the real intent of hitting higher than the fake.
8. Fake Right - Attack Left	Motion to the right with the head, body, hand, leg, or a combination of these with the real intent of hitting the left.
9. Fake Left - Attack Right	Motion to the left with the head, body, hand, leg, or a combination of these with the real intent of hitting the right.
8. In And Out Draw	Make motions toward the opponent and then quickly move back away, meant to draw the opponent in.
9. Fake Turn	Begin to turn the body as if to throw a spinning kick or spinning backfist and then come back to the original position with an attack.
10. Foot Fakes	Draw the opponent's attention to the feet with a fake kick or other movement and then hit with either punch or another kick.
11. Body One Direction - Technique Another	Draw the opponent's attention to the torso by moving it one way and throw an attack from another angle.
12. In-Between Fakes	Throw a kick or punch, insert some kind of fake (hand, foot, head, etc.), and immediately throw another technique.
13. Rapping	Slaps and hits on the opponent's arms or hands to distract the opponent or temporarily freeze the opponent in order to land a technique.
14. Pestering	Being obnoxious in movement and intent aimed to frustrate the opponent, in order to break his concentration. *Can take many different forms.*
15. Radical Moves	Movements that don't really look like typical techniques but can become a technique. Example, a *wild spinning backfist that looks more like a helicopter propeller.*
16 Psyche-Talk.	Conversation with the opponent designed to break his concentration or to give him a false sense of self. Example; "*I can never hope to beat you, you're too good!*"
17. Fake Body Language	Faking injuries, faking fatigue, faking frustration, or any other emotion that will cause the opponent to think he has an advantage.
17. Taunting	Verbal harassment of the opponent in order to break his concentration or to evoke an emotional response.
18. Intentional Telegraphing	Using movements or motions that are normally considered "telegraphing" to cause the opponent to attack.

19. Reputation	What other fighters know, or have heard about another fighter can influence how two fighters compete against each other. Some fighters have a specialty, like fast kicks and they are known for this.
20. Fake Emotions	Showing false emotions such as anger, fear, frustration, etc. in order to make the opponent think you're feeling this way when actually you're focused and confident.

Rules Tactics

1. Stalling	Purposefully avoiding the opponent in order to run the clock down.
2. Going Out Of Bounds	Going out of bounds so that the action will stop and the opponent can't hit you.
3. Injury	When injured during competition use it to gain time, or fake an injury (not recommended).
4. Time Outs	Use time-outs at the appropriate time. If the rules allow them.
5. Time Between Rounds	Use the time between rounds to rest but also to do more planning.

Attribute Tactics

1. Broken Rhythm	Ability to change the pace and timing of footwork, techniques, and other aspects of fighting with the goal of confusing the opponent.
2. Speed	Change - increase or decrease speed in attacks and defense. To be faster than the opponent.
3. Power	Change - increase or decrease in the amount of power used in attacks and defense. To use more power than the opponent.
4. Timing	Ability to execute techniques with the proper form and at the proper time.
5. Precision	Hitting exactly what you intended to hit.

6. Mobility	Ability to use footwork to ones advantage. To control the pace and fighting range of the fight.
7. Endurance	Ability to fight and not become tired. Tire out the opponent.
8. Reaction Time	Ability to react and execute a proper response, the ability to react to change. React faster than the opponent.
9. Toughness	The ability to endure more than the opponent.
10. Height	Ability to use height to an advantage.
11. Weight	Ability to use weight to an advantage.
12. Reach	Able to reach the opponent without the opponent reaching you
13. Technique Choice	Able to choose the correct techniques at the appropriate time.
14. No-Mind	Pure reaction, attack or defend without pre-thought -- automatic action.

Non-Specific Tactics

1. Angling	Using angles in various ways, with hand and foot techniques, and also in movement.
2. Centering	Using the centerline (a vertical line that divides the body in half) to guide ones attack and/or defense.
3. Grappling (Grab)	Various forms of grabbing, from those meant to distract the opponent to those meant to lock a joint or choke.
4. Sticking	Using touch as a guide to hitting or defending.
5. Trapping	Various ways of causing the opponent from using his arm or leg by not allowing him to move it - pinning it against his body or your body. (Different from a grab)
6. No-Recovery	Using the idea of once a technique has been used (either an attack or a defensive technique) don't recover it, but change it into another technique from its extended position.
7. Broken Rhythm	Using an inconsistent timing in movement or technique execution - being unpredictable.
8. Probing	Pressuring the opponent with movement and fakes in order to see how he responds.
9. Hit And Run	Attack the opponent and then quickly move out of his counter attack range.
10. Charge	Race at the opponent, with either and attack a defensive move or combinations.

11. Sweeps	Disrupt the opponent's balance with a sweeping motion to his legs - usually done with legs.
12. Locks	Various ways of immobilizing the joints.
13. Pressure	Various ways of making the opponent feel uncomfortable, from psyche talk, charging, trapping, rapping, etc.
14. Radical Moves	Using a technique, movement, or combination of techniques and movement that are executed with bad form. Usually in the form of exaggeration - to break the opponent's concentration.
15. Changing Tactics	Going quickly from one tactic to another, to keep the opponent guessing.
16. Off-Balancing	Various ways of disrupting the opponent's balance from pushing, rapping, sweeping, etc.
17. Nerve Hits	Either defending or attacking by hitting the nerves causing the opponent pain, numbness, or unconsciousness.
18. Half-Grapples	Various ways of controlling the opponent's limbs or head or repositioning the opponent's limbs or head leading into a full grappling move, joint lock, push, throw, hit, etc.
19. Changing Styles	Change to a whole different system of fighting in order to confuse the opponent, and to use that system's tactical advantages.
20. Forward Pressure	When touching the opponent with the hands, wrist, or forearms having a sense of forward pressure that would create a springing forward towards the opponent if no resistance were there.

Chapter Thirteen

"Your commitment may be tested. Credibility must be earned."

Avinsh K. Dixit &
Barry J. Nalebuff

Becoming A Superior Fighter

If you were asked to define what a superior fighter is how would you do it? Would you use a fighter's win and loss record or the fact that someone is a champion? To wear the title "superior" how many fights does someone need to win? What if a fighter knocks out the champion in his very first fight? Is he a superior fighter? Is the Grand Master of your style a superior fighter just because he's the Grand Master? There must be some way to identify a "good" or "superior" fighter?

Until the inception of the A.Y.F.M., defining what a "superior" fighter has depended more on personal opinion than on any scientific measurements. Since the A.Y.F.M. allows you to appraise how martial artists fight and transpose their fighting into numbers (such as scoring percentages), establishing a clear definition of a superior fighter is possible.

The A.Y.F.M. defines a superior fighter as a fighter who has a **Skill Quotient** above 51%. The next chapter contains a full explanation of the Skill Quotient and how it is used. Preceding the definition of the Skill Quotient is an examination of the various characteristics of a superior fighter.

Characteristics Of The Superior Fighter

The Superior Fighter Understands Fighting:

Let's examine fighting or sparring in a critical manner and apply it to what makes a superior fighter. Fighting on the physical level contains two basic elements, techniques and movement. All martial arts styles or systems are built upon this basic structure, that techniques are used to hit, throw, choke, grab, etc., while movement is needed to either land the techniques in an offensive sense or to evade, avoid, or counter the opponent in a defensive sense.

Along with technique and movement, fighting also involves various mental aspects such as fear, confidence, etc. All of these aspects, techniques, movement, and mental fortitude are perpetuated in various forms of training. Martial artists train vigorously on their technique, movement, and understanding of the psychology of fighting.

Therefore, a superior martial artist first develops both good technique and movement, and then the mental strength to use strategy to apply tactics in a consistent manner that greatly increases his chances of winning.

The superior fighter also understands that only four things can occur during a fight:

1. Change in technique.
2. Change in tactic.
3. Change in emotions, feelings, and attitude.
4. Loss of efficiency or inability to act because of injury, exhaustion, fear, etc.

The Superior Fighter Knows What Is Primary and What Is Secondary In Fighting:

Primary		*Secondary*
Reading or seeing motion.	*Versus*	Reading or seeing techniques.
Controlling the distance or "range."	*Versus*	Hitting.
Affecting the opponent's mind.	*Versus*	Affecting the opponent's body.
Controlling the pace.	*Versus*	Attributes.

Your reactions are too slow to see everything as "technique" so reading motion is more important than recognizing individual techniques as you fight. The superior fighter sees what occurs before techniques are thrown; reading the opponent's set-point, seeing slight changes in his stance or arm and leg position (as if setting up a specific counter), or recognizing facial expressions that mean an attack is coming, etc. The superior fighter can react before an attack just as easily as he can react during an attack or after an attack.

The superior fighter also knows that it's more important to control the distance or "range" during a fight than to be concerned with just hitting. Once you control the "range," than you can pick and choose how and when you land techniques.

Landing techniques is often secondary to affecting the opponent's mind. For once doubt takes over the opponent's thoughts his concentration falters and you have essentially defeated him. There are many ways to break the opponent's concentration causing the opponent to have a negative emotional reaction, such as frustration. Weaken the opponent's mind and you've weakened his response.

Along with controlling the range and affecting the mind, the superior fighter knows that controlling the "pace" of the fight is primary to having some type of advantage caused by "attributes." That is, even if an opponent is taller than you and has a longer reach, if you control the "pace" of the fight you can affect how he uses his attributes. If you move and execute at a faster pace than the opponent for example, you prevent the opponent from having a comfort zone in which to use his advantages.

By knowing what is primary and what is secondary in fighting, the superior fighter sets the rules of engagement.

The Superior Fighter Understands The FourRanges Of Attack

1. **Kicking Range:**	Since the legs have a farther reach than the arms, the farthest away that you can be to your opponent and still land a technique is the kicking range. This is not to say that kicks can't be used in other ranges.
2. **Hand Range:**	This is the distance from the opponent in which you can land punching techniques.
3. **Elbow/Knee Range:**	This is the distance from the opponent in which you can land elbow and knee techniques. Also included in this range would be head-butts, and shoulder hits, etc.
4. **Grappling Range:**	This is the distance from the opponent in which joint locks and choking techniques are employed. This range is also associated with grappling techniques employed on the ground.

Note: This range breakdown is not universally accepted by all practitioners.

The Superior Fighter Understands Discipline:

You can't be a superior fighter without embracing these aspects of discipline:

- Severely focused on a clear goal.
- Relentless effort in practice, and in the search for knowledge and experience.
- Self-knowledge - know yourself very well (analyze your fighting often).

Important Keys To Being A Superior Fighter

♦ Becoming a superior fighter is not a simple thing; it's a long and involved process of learning the reality of fighting and the human emotional response to it. The above "to do" list is the fighter's "credo." Fighters should live everyday in pursuit of "doing" what this list represents. Being a *superior martial artist* is a way of life not a part time hobby. Principles and convictions drive and motivate the superior martial artist not feelings and emotions. Reason has to be in charge of the superior martial artist's soul. Win/loss records aren't as important to defining the superior martial artist as identifying and achieving one's goals and doing it with character! The "art" in modern martial arts is taking the creative leap to using the benefits of training to express one's uniqueness. The superior fighter moves away from being a "type" of fighter and becomes a "unique" fighter.

♦ The superior fighter often stays one step ahead of the opponent. He rarely fights from being behind in terms of points or any other aspect of fighting. He understands that whoever "controls" the fight sets himself up for victory. Even if the superior fighter isn't a very aggressive fighter, he's still seeking control by appearing passive. For the superior fighter knows that it's the aggressor who defines the "rules" of the engagement and he "picks" when he wants to score and more often than not he does.

♦ The superior fighter is able to balance reaction with thinking. His thoughts don't hinder his reactions -- emotions never take over his thoughts. The superior fighter uses his thinking and interpretation skills to read the signals that his opponent is sending. As he interprets the opponent's intentions, he uses tactics that are part of a pre-fight strategy. At the same time, he's able to fight as if he had "no-mind," to let the trained reactions that are a part of his nervous system take over without the time consuming mechanisms of reasoning.

♦ Many superior fighters are specialists, that is, they are extremely good at some aspect of fighting such as kicking. You may want to consider developing a specialty as an integral part of your abilities. Specialty fighters create fear and apprehension in opponents by the very fact that they're specialists. Specialty fighters use their reputation as an important tactic. If you're going to compete than people are going to talk about you. Become a performer not just a fighter. This doesn't mean become an arrogant egocentric dramatic actor, but be aware of how you can influence what others say about you. Become someone who's respected and admired!

♦ Don't let the concepts of tactics and strategies convince you that fighting is all about trying to control everything that happens in a fight -- the wonder of it all is in spontaneity. The fascination with fighting is to breach the unknown. But, winning has a clear path, and it takes meticulous planning and preparation to be a fighter. The superior fighter can meet the spontaneous with skill to spare.

♦ The superior fighter wants to be unpredictable, not only to his opponents but even to himself. To create new movements and tactics as he fights. To react to opponents in new more intense motions and emotions? To grow as he spars or competes, never just wanting to "get through it?"

♦ The superior fighter is both a strategist and a tactician. A strategist plans ahead, using information from research and past experience to plot how he will fight certain opponents. A tactician uses the correct tactics to adapt to the constantly changing conditions of a fight. A technician is someone who just throws techniques and makes little use of tactics or strategies -- kind of a "try this and see what happens" method. It's the strategist and the technician who truly understand fighting! The technician is not as advanced as the strategist and tactician. The superior fighter makes it all work!

♦ Above all else, a superior fighter is a consistent performer -- maintaining his execution, attitude, and training. The superior fighter knows that improvement can only come from consistency. Therefore, his focus is on becoming better, not just maintaining his skills.

The Superior Fighter Has:
The will to do. The discipline to do.
The confidence to do. The knowledge to do.
The experience to do.

The 80-20 Rule

The 80-20 Rule sheds an intriguing light on human behavior, particularly when it comes to martial arts. Let's say you have an advanced word processor for your computer and have spent time studying the hundreds of pages in the manual that explains how to use all the wonderful features of the program. Then you spend many hours learning how to use the program. After studying the manual and working with the software, you still don't know everything about the capabilities of the program especially the advanced features. So, with all there is to know about the program, you have learned 80% of it. Then of all the knowledge that you have of the program (80% of the total) you probably only use about 20% of what you know on a regular basis as you create documents.

Now apply this analogy to the martial arts. Unless you're the rare individual who knows the total system or style of martial art that you study, you're probably like the majority of martial artists who fall somewhere close to the *80-20 Rule*. That is, you may know 80% of the system, but can only apply with proficiency and consistency 20% of what you know in actual fighting or sparring. This is just a part of human nature, and explains why becoming proficient in the martial arts takes such a long time. People are prone to doing what they enjoy, what they're good at, and to doing the same things over and over again.

The superior fighter will defy the *80-20 Rule* by coming very close to knowing and being able to use his whole system of martial arts. That is, he can apply a greater variety of martial arts techniques and tactics than the average martial artist.

The 20-80 Rule

The *20-80 Rule* is another interesting way to look at how most fighters use techniques. The rule states that 20% of all the possible techniques in the martial arts are used 80% of the time. This should become very clear to you after doing several analyses -- that of all the techniques that you learn you only use a small fraction of them when it comes time to fight. This is partly due in competition to rules that limit what techniques you can use, and also because most martial artists find confidence in using a small number of techniques. It's difficult to branch out and use different techniques when you don't have confidence in your ability to score with them.

The superior fighter wants to break away from the *20-80 Rule* as much as possible. He doesn't want to be limited in his approach to fighting.

The Fighters' Quotient

As this chapter has already made clear, the superior fighter has many qualities related to his advanced level of skill, conditioning, and reasoning. Since the A.Y.F.M. allows you to translate most aspects of fighting into numbers and percentages, a certain set of these numbers can be averaged together to "score" or "rate" a fighter's overall ability according to a chart. This score is called *The Fighters' Quotient*, and the chart that rates a fighter is appropriately called *The Fighters' Ability Rating Chart*. The chart places fighters in four categories of ability, with the highest rating on the chart representing the **Superior Fighter**.

There are three aspects of fighting that are averaged together to calculate *The Fighters' Quotient*, which are listed below:

1. The Win/Loss Percentage	The number of wins as compared to the number of loses.
2. Scoring Percentage	The number of techniques that scored as compared to the number of techniques thrown.
3. Technique Usage Percentage	Of all the legal practical techniques allowed in a competition, the number that a fighter can score with.

These three categories are the most important factors in explaining why someone is a winner. The win/loss record alone is not descriptive enough. Adding to the win/loss record the scoring percentage and technique usage percentage gives a more complete picture of a fighter's ability. A fighter is rated according to his ability to win, to score, and to score with a variety of techniques.

Determining A Fighter's Rating

To rate yourself fairly you need to have analyzed at least ten fights. Do not use a mixture of tournament and sparring fights. Use either ten tournament fights or ten sparring fights. The sparring sessions should also be consistent in make-up. They should consist of the same number of timed rounds against opponents of the same rank or comparable in skill. Don't mix in fights with inferior opponents and superior opponents. You should also use ten different opponents. After you have the numbers from ten fights (meaning you've completed a personal fighting database), you'll need to figure the averages of your win/loss percentage, scoring percentage, and technique usage percentage for the ten fights. Use your personal fighting database and follow these steps:

1. Divide the number of fights you had with the number you won.

   7 wins ÷ 10 fights x 100 = 70%

2. Average your scoring percentages over the ten fights.

Fight	Scoring Percentage
Fight #1 =	27%
Fight #2 =	24%
Fight #3 =	22%
Fight #4 =	26%
Fight #5 =	28%
Fight #6 =	33%

Fight #7 = 31%
Fight #8 = 27%
Fight #9 = 22%
Fight #10 = 27%
             267 Total

Total number of the above percentages = 267.

Divide 267 by the total number of fights or 10.

267 ÷ 10 = 26.7%

3. List all the legal practical techniques that you can use in competition, such as front kick, back fist, etc. Only include "practical" techniques in your list. For example, in kick-boxing it may be legal to do a flying side kick, but it's not practical and therefore not likely that any fighter will fly across the ring.

Count how many of the legal practical techniques you're able to score with. It's a common thread among great fighters that they can use a variety of techniques. Most competitions include about 15 legal techniques. This example uses 15 as the number of usable techniques and 10 as the number of techniques used to score with. Now figure the percentage of techniques used to score as compared to allowed techniques.

10 ÷ 15 x 100 = 67%

4. Now add the three percentages together and find the average score;

Win/Loss	= 70%
Scoring	= 26.7%
Technique usage	= 67%
	163.7 ÷ 3 = 54.6% Fighter's Quotient

5. Use the fighter's quotient from above and compare that score to the chart below to find the fighters rating.

Fighters' Ability Rating Chart

Once you have found the average of your win/loss percentage, the scoring percentage, and the technique usage percentage for at least ten fights, you can rate your fighting ability according to the chart below.

A poor rating would illustrate the lack of a fighter's ability to win fights, to score, and to score with a variety of different techniques. Most fighters fall in the average range on the chart. That is, they win a number of fights, are able to score with good consistency, and can use a number of different techniques.

Since the fighters' ability rating isn't dependent on a fighter's win/loss record alone, a high scoring percentage and technique usage percentage in a losing fight can still help a fighter's rating. For there are times when you score with a high percentage of the techniques that you throw and with a variety of techniques, but you still lose. On the other hand, you could also win a fight and have a low scoring percentage and only use one or two different techniques. The following chart reflects the fact that a good fighter is a consistent fighter who wins often, scores with most of the techniques he throws, and can score with a variety of techniques.

Fighters' Ability Rating Chart

Rating	Score
Poor	0 - 29%
Average	30 - 40%
Expert	41 - 50%
Superior	51 - 100%

Conclusion

Achieving a superior rating is a very difficult thing to do. It's representative of any high achievement in sport, comparable to receiving a gold medal at the Olympics. It's an honor that only the unique martial artist will achieve!

Chapter Fourteen

Analyze Your Fighting Method
Worksheets

The A.Y.F.M. contains twelve different worksheets. This chapter contains all eleven worksheets ready for you to copy and use.

Make as many copies of the worksheets as you need. Most of the time you'll need more than one copy of the worksheet you're using in order to analyze a fight.

The worksheets used as examples throughout the book are designed for point karate, kick-boxing, or boxing. Modify any of the worksheets when it's necessary to adapt them to your particular type of competition.

Worksheet	Description
1. Technique Breakdown Worksheet #1	Basic Information And Pre-analysis Interpretation
2. Technique Breakdown Worksheet #2	Technique Usage
3. Technique Breakdown Worksheet #3	Movement, Reaction, Combination
4. Level One Evaluation	Discovering Trends In Your Fighting
5. Level Two Evaluation	Winning Or Losing A Particular Fight
6. Level Three Evaluation	Technical & Tactical Evaluation
7. Level Four Evaluation	Fighter Comparison Worksheet
8. Level Five Evaluation	Retrospection Breakdown
9. Level Five Evaluation	Retrospection Summary
10. Workout Plan	Planning Workouts
11. Strategy Worksheet	Forming Strategies
12. Mixed Martial Artist Worksheet	Compare Mixed Martial Artist Fighters

TECHNIQUE BREAKDOWN WORKSHEET #1
Basic Information & Pre-Analysis Interpretation

Tape #: _____ Counter #: _____ Analysis #: _____

Tournament Or Sparring Session: _____ Date: _____

Score: Fighter #1: _____ Fighter #2: _____

Analysis Done By: _____ Date: _____

Fighter #1: _____

School: _____ Style: _____ Rank: _____

Height: _____ Weight: _____ Age: _____

Fighter #2: _____

School: _____ Style: _____ Rank: _____

Height: _____ Weight: _____ Age: _____

Pre-Analysis Interpretation:

How did you feel that day before you fought? _____

How did you feel about your conditioning? _____

Do you feel you were judged fairly? Why or why not?_____

What is your perception of what happened? Why did you win or lose? _____

_____

Were there noticeable differences in strength, speed, etc.? _____

_____

What do you need to improve on? _____

_____

What was your pre-fight strategy and did it work? _____

_____

Notes:

_____

TECHNIQUE BREAKDOWN WORKSHEET #2
Technique Usage

Analysis #: _____ Round(s): _____   Fighter's Name: _____

Tournament Or Sparring Session: _____   Opponent: _____

Breakdown Codes:

Score = S	High = (Leave Blank)	Right = R	Bad Call = BC	Jammed = JM
Penalty = P	Medium = M	Left = L	Knockout = KO	Round = \\
Warning = W	Low = X	Note = N	Terrible = T	Divides Technique = \
Counter Punch = CP	Clash = C	Faint/Fake = F	Jumping = J	Blocked = B

Punches:	Totals:	Left	Right	Right & Left	Score
1. Backfist:					
2. Reverse (Cross):					
3. Front (Jab):					
4. Ridge Hand:					
5. Hook					
6. Upper Cut:					
7					
8.					
Punching Totals:					

Kicks:	Totals:	Left	Right	Right & Left	Score
1. Front:					
2. Side:					
3. Roundhouse:					
4. Hook:					
5. Crescent					
6. Spinning:					
7. Axe:					
8. Back Kick:					
9.					
Kicking Totals:					
GRAND TOTALS:					

TECHNIQUE BREAKDOWN WORKSHEET #3
Movement, Reaction, Combinations

Analysis #: _____ Round(s): _____   Fighter's Name: _____

Tournament Or Sparring Session: _____   Opponent: _____

Movement Breakdown:

	Total		Total
Attack =		Counter Punch (CP) =	
Backward (BW) =		Block Or Perry (BP) =	
Defend =		Circling =	
Stood Ground (SG) =		Left (L) =	
Foot Fake =		Right (R) =	
Hand Fake =		Cover (CO) =	
Stance Switch =		Turning Away =	
Body Fake =		Spin =	

Reaction To The Opponent Breakdown:

Opponent: _____

Your Reaction: _____

Opponent: _____

Your Reaction: _____

Opponent: _____

Your Reaction: _____

Notes: _____

Total Blocked: _____   Total Avoided: _____   Total Countered: _____

Combination Log: _____

_____

_____

_____

Notes: _____

Total Hand Combinations: _____   Total Foot Combinations: _____   Total Hand & Foot: _____

Technique Codes:

Back Fist = BF	Reverse Punch = RP	Cross = C	Cover = CO	Elbow = E
Jab = J	Hook = H	Upper Cut = UC	Ridge Hand = RH	Knee = K
Palm Strike = PS	Shuto = S	Forearm = FO	Shoulder = SD	Head Butt = HB
Grab = G	Roundhouse = RK	Ax Kick = AK	Back Kick = BK	Spinning Kick = Add S
Sweep = SW	Grab = G	Front Kick = FK	Side Kick = SK	Sweep = SW
Fake = F				

Discovering Your Fighting Trends
Level One Evaluation

Trend Evaluation:

Behavior and/or comparison: _____

Time period or number of fights: _____

Frequency: _____

Positive or negative affects of this trend on performance: _____
_____
_____
_____

Goal(s) for improving or changing this trend:

1.	
2.	
3.	
4.	

Training ideas & notes:

Trend Evaluation:

Behavior and/or comparison: _____

Time period or number of fights: _____

Frequency: _____

Positive or negative effects of this trend on performance: _____
_____
_____
_____

Goal(s) for improving or changing this trend:

1.	
2.	
3.	
4.	

Training ideas & notes:

Winning Or Losing A Particular Fight
Level Two Evaluation

Tape #: _____ Counter #: _____ Analysis #: _____

Fighter #1: _____ Score: _____
Fighter #2: _____ Score: _____

1. This evaluation is being done to discover why you: A). Won _____ B). Lost _____ C.) Other
_____

2. List the positive and negative aspects of your perfomance in each of the categories below:
(Use another worksheet if you wish to list these aspects of your opponent's performance.)

Body Type: *Positive*
1. _____
2. _____
3. _____

Body Type: *Negative*
1. _____
2. _____
3. _____

Attributes: *Positive*
1. _____
2. _____
3. _____
4. _____
5. _____

Attributes: *Negative*
1. _____
2. _____
3. _____
4. _____
5. _____

Technique & Tactic Usage: *Positive*
1. _____
2. _____
3. _____
4. _____
5. _____

Technique & Tactic Usage: *Negative*
1. _____
2. _____
3. _____
4. _____
5. _____

Mental Skills: *Positive*
1. _____
2. _____
3. _____
4. _____
5. _____

Mental Skills: *Negative*
1. _____
2. _____
3. _____
4. _____
5. _____

3. Did your fight strategy work? Why or why not?

4. Who controlled the pace and why?

5. Who controlled the distance and why?

6. Conclusion as to why you won, lost, or other?

7. Training ideas and/or notes:

Technical & Tactical Evaluation
Level Three Evaluation

Name: _____ Date: _____

Tape # _____ Counter # _____ Analysis # (s) _____

1. This evaluation is based on how many fights? _____

2. What are you evaluating or comparing? _____

_____

3. Is it technically correct? Why or why not? _____

_____

_____

4. What are the strong points and weak points in the following attributes of what you are evaluationg?

Speed: _____

Power: _____

Timing: _____

Mobility: _____

Precision: _____

Endurance: _____

Focus: _____

Recovery: _____

5. What tactics do you use to land these techniques and are they effective? Why or why not?

_____

_____

_____

_____

Notes:

Fighter Comparison Worksheet
Level Four Evaluation

Reason(s) You Are Using This Fighter For Comparison: _____

Fighter's Names:	1.	2.
Number Of Fights Analyzed ForComparison?		
Scoring % Kicks & Punches:		
Scoring % Kicks:		
Scoring % Hands:		
Total Punches Thrown:		
Total Kicks Thrown:		
Movement:(Attacks & Defenses)		
Combinations:		
Most Commonly Used Offensive Tactic?		
Most Commonly Used Defensive Tactic?		
Attributes: Strengths?		
Attributes: Weaknesses?		
Explain Fighters Use Of Tactics & Strategy?		
How Does The Fighter Use Distance?		
How Does The Fighter Use Pace?		
What Areas Of Fighting Does The Fighter Specialize In?		
Emphasis Of Training?(Style, Etc.)		

General Conclusions (Training Ideas, Etc.):

Retrospection Worksheet
Level Five Evaluation Breakdown

Name: _____ Date: _____

Tape #: _____ Counter #: _____ Analysis #: _____

Tournament: _____ Sparring: _____ Event: _____

Opponent: _____

Round: _____ **Attack:** _____ **Defense:** _____

Before: (Thought or Feeling) _____
        (Tactic) _____

During: (Thought or Feeling) _____
        (Tactic) _____

After: (Thought or Feeling) _____
        (Tactic) _____

Round: _____ **Attack:** _____ **Defense:** _____

Before: (Thought or Feeling) _____
        (Tactic) _____

During: (Thought or Feeling) _____
        (Tactic) _____

After: (Thought or Feeling) _____
        (Tactic) _____

Round: _____ **Attack:** _____ **Defense:** _____

Before: (Thought or Feeling) _____
        (Tactic) _____

During: (Thought or Feeling) _____
        (Tactic) _____

After: (Thought or Feeling) _____
        (Tactic) _____

Round: _____ **Attack:** _____ **Defense:** _____

Before: (Thought or Feeling) _____
        (Tactic) _____

During: (Thought or Feeling) _____
        (Tactic) _____

After: (Thought or Feeling) _____
        (Tactic) _____

Retrospection Worksheet
Level Five Evaluation Summary

Name: _____ Date: _____

Tape #: _____ Counter #: _____ Analysis #: _____

Tournament: _____ Sparring: _____ Event: _____

Opponent(s): _____

1. Summarize your dominant feeling(s) or emotion(s) as you fight?

Before: _____

During: _____

After: _____

Cause: _____

2. Summarize your dominant thoughts as you fight?

Before: _____

During: _____

After: _____

Cause: _____

3. Summarize your dominant tactical responses while attacking?

a. _____

b. _____

c. _____

4. Summarize your dominant tactical responses while defending?

a. _____

b. _____

c _____

5. Summarize what your body language and facial expressions are showing?

Before: _____

During: _____

After: _____

Cause: _____

6. Did you have any pre-fight, environmental, post-fight, etc. concerns that may have impacted your performance?

7. How did you prepare yourself mentally while training? Did it help you during competition? Why or why not?

8. How did you prepare yourself mentally the day of the fight? Did it help you during competition? Why or why not?

9. Make a list of the areas you need to improve on?

Training Ideas:

Workout Plan

Name: _____ Date: _____ Workout #: _____

Ultimate Goal: _____

Main objective(s): At the completion of _____ training sessions I will have learned, or be able to do, know, etc. the following;

1. _____

2. _____

3. _____

Objective(s) for this workout:

1. _____

2. _____

3. _____

	Time:	Exercises & Drills:
1.		
2.		
3.		
4.		
5.		
6.		
7.		
8.		
9.		
10.		

Evaluation: _____

_____

Materials Needed:

Reference Material:

Strategy Worksheet

Your Name: _____   Opponent's Name: _____
Style: _____   Style: _____

Type Of Fighter	You	Opponent	Range Preferences	You	Opponent
Offensive			Hand		
Defensive			Kicking		
Other			Elbow/Knee		
Other			Grappling		

Your Tactical Preferences:

1. _____

2. _____

3. _____

Your Movement Patterns:

_____

_____

Opponent's Tactical Preferences:

1. _____

2. _____

3. _____

Opponent's Movement Patterns:

_____

_____

Your Attributes	Strengths	Weaknesses
Speed		
Power		
Timing		
Flexibility		
Conditioning		
Body Type		
Other		

Opponent's Attributes	Strengths	Weaknesses
Speed		
Power		
Timing		
Flexibility		
Conditioning		
Body Type		
Other		

Your Mental Disposition:

_____

Opponent's Mental Disposition:

_____

Additional Information About Opponent:

Formulate Your Strategy Below:

Personal Fighting Database

Tournament: _____ **Sparring:** _____

Analysis #	1.	2.	3.	Block #1 Totals #1-3.	4.	5.	6.	Block #2 Totals #4-6	Totals #1 & 2
Your Score:									
Opponent's Score:									
Opponent's Weight:									
Opponent's Height:									
Total Scoring Percentage Hands:				Average				Average	Average
Total Scoring Percentage Kicks:				Average				Average	Average
Total Punches:									
Total Kicks:									
Total Punches & Kicks:									
Total Punches & Kicks Scoring Percentage:				Average				Average	Average
Most Frequent Punch Name:									
Most Frequent Kick Name:									
Movement: Attack									
Defend									
Fakes									
Backwards									
Combinations: Hand									
Foot									
Hand & Foot									
Combinations Scored:									
Reaction: Blocked									
Avoided									
Countered									

Mixed Martial Arts Worksheet

Fighter #1: _____

Height: _____
Weight: _____
Reach: _____
Age: _____
Stance: _____
Fight Record: Win: _____ Loss: _____
             Draw: _____ Knockout: _____

Stand-Up

Strengths: _____

_____

_____

Weaknesses: _____

_____

_____

Ground Game

Strengths: _____

_____

_____

Weaknesses: _____

_____

_____

Transition Game

Strengths: _____

_____

_____

Weaknesses: _____

_____

_____

Fighter #2: _____

Height: _____
Weight: _____
Reach: _____
Age: _____
Stance: _____
Fight Record: Win: _____ Loss: _____
             Draw: _____ Knockout: _____

Stand-Up

Strengths: _____

_____

_____

Weaknesses: _____

_____

_____

Ground Game

Strengths: _____

_____

_____

Weaknesses: _____

_____

_____

Transition Game

Strengths: _____

_____

_____

Weaknesses: _____

_____

_____

About The Author

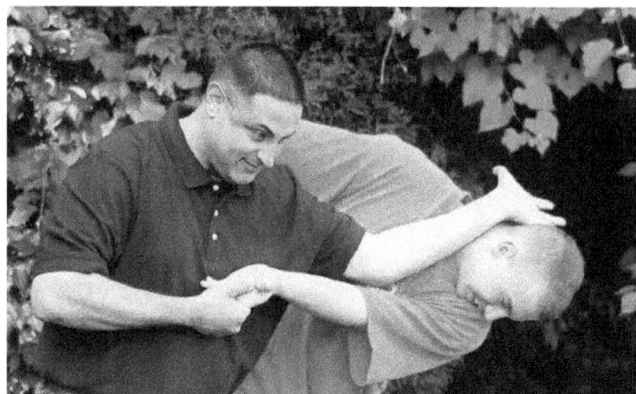

Darin Waugh

A product of the Bruce Lee explosion of the 70's, **Darin Waugh** began training in the martial arts after seeing a Bruce Lee movie at a drive in theater in 1976.

His martial arts career is sprinkled with a little bit of everything; besides teaching and competing he has also been involved in producing independent action movies, co-founded Eclectic Bujutsu (a multi-art organization), and helped host the annual tribute event Bruce Lee Eve.

Mr. Waugh graduated from The Ohio State University (OSU) in 1988 with a Bachelor of Science degree in health education. While at OSU, Mr. Waugh trained at and became an instructor for the famed Do-Jung-Ishu Club. He spent over twenty years with Do-Jung-Ishu training hundreds of students and developing his own personal expression of martial arts called, Sticky Boxing.

Currently, as of 2012, Mr. Waugh is studying Keysi Fighting Method, at KFM Charlotte in Charlotte, North Carolina. He also continues to work on various martial arts writing projects through his publishing company Kiazen Publications.

Mr. Waugh believes in emphasizing both the practical application of martial arts techniques (to meet the reality of fighting) and the "art" in martial arts to create innovative ways to practice and employ the martial arts.

Contact Mr. Waugh for seminars on **Sticky Boxing** and **Analyze Your Fighting** at JKDMan@aol.com or on his Face book page at https://www.facebook.com/darin.waugh?ref=tn_tnmn !

Other books by Darin Waugh are available at: http://www.lulu.com/spotlight/dman2x .